ANCHOR BOOKS

INSPIRATIONS FROM THE

SOUTH EAST

Edited by

David Foskett

First published in Great Britain in 1996 by
ANCHOR BOOKS
1-2 Wainman Road, Woodston,
Peterborough, PE2 7BU

HB ISBN 1 85930 328 5
SB ISBN 1 85930 323 4

Foreword

Anchor Books is a small press, established in 1992, with the aim of promoting readable poetry to as wide an audience as possible.

The poems in *Inspirations From the South East* represent a cross-section of style and content.

These poems are written by young and old alike, united in their passion for writing poetry.

I trust this selection will delight and please the authors from the *South East* and all those who enjoy reading poetry.

David Foskett
Editor

CONTENTS

MY GARDEN

A garden full of flowers
Where you can while away the hours
Is a garden filled with pleasure.
To watch the birds and bees at leisure
The bees fly to and fro
To gather pollen as they go.
The birds are gaily singing, each thinking he is best
While other little feathered friends, are busy with their nest.
The flowers all in their splendour
With fragrant perfumes they do render.
The stately trees stand straight and tall
And wait until the autumn fall.
A garden has so many things
That grow, and sing, and fly with wings.

P L Todd

TWO LITTLE HANDS (A GHOST STORY)

Someone has turned on the tap in the kitchen -
I'll go to the door, but I know what I'll see.
Two pretty white hands that are turning and twisting -
The water runs over them - clear as can be.

Sometimes they're dusty, from sweeping the hallway,
And sometimes they're dirty, from carrying coal,
And once, she was washing a cut on her finger -
I'm sure she was crying - the poor little soul.

Maybe I ought to tell someone about her,
But who in the wide world would ever believe,
That there at the tap, at the sink, in the kitchen,
Are two little hands - that stop short - at the sleeve!

Brenda Baker

REMEMBER THIS FOR DAYS TO COME

Remember this for days to come
You are loved by someone true
But rain it will from time to time
As much as I wish for skies blue.
There's always a cloud that wanders amongst
Those beautiful golden rays
But underneath these showers, I know
I can see past the dusty haze.
Challenge this is you believe not
I'll return with a beautiful sigh
This amazing gift I have, I give
Think deep before passing it by.
The colours of love, the richest there are
So flowing from every thought
The breath of love is what I hold
My true love is what you've caught.

J J Henry

THE LONELY ROSE

In the morning mist I chanced to see
A pale pink rose 'neath the old elm tree.
It had shed a tear so crystal bright,
Rainbow colours reflecting the light.
Oh pale pink rose, why have you cried?
The other roses have faded and died.
Are you lonely under the old elm tree?
Lonely and sad, the same as me?

Eva Loncke

SNOW

The leaden skies hang grey like death,
Below, the cold sees people's breath.
Hurrying, scurrying 'ere I fall,
Before they reach their port of call.

Above the earth, my time I bide,
'Til God sees fit for me to glide
Downward, dancing feathers white,
Weightless, silent, serene not quite
The awesome winter cover,
But more, the earth's so fleeting lover.

Hated, dreaded, feared, 'tis true,
My beauty scorned by all of you.
For I care not where I alight,
O'er field or wood or building site.
Where man has been and left such taint,
For me so gently now to paint,
With strokes of white, pure filigree
Caress each twig, each bough, each tree.

'Til Mother Nature lights her fire,
The sun - alas! My funeral pyre.
My beauty blackened slips away,
And waits on high for skies of grey.

Nola J McSweeney

TRAVEL PASS

When Ernest Picklethwaite went to sea
It weren't in pea green boat.
It were with wife Elsie, her mum Glad,
And old friend Winnie Scrote

They never took to foreign parts
It wasn't quite their style
As Ernest oft was hear to say
'What's wrong with Golden Mile!'

Now Ernest worked for British Rail
It meant a job for life
It also gave a special pass
Just for him like, and the wife

To get good value with his pass
They should have gone for miles
But Ma-in-law, and Winnie too
Would not have been all smiles

So dreams of Blackpool, Newquay too
Were not things they could act on
They knew that every bloomin' year
They'd all end up at Clacton

The sad result of all of this
Just to keep the women sweet
Meant holidays, like workdays too
Were Clacton from Liverpool Street

R Arnold Comben

THE HOP PICKERS

Life is so different, now down in Kent,
For the hop pickers came, and then they went.
This was all before hops were picked by machines,
Alas now hop picking days are all *has beens*.
They came by the thousand to pick all the hops,
And had Saturdays off to go to the shops.
The ate round camp fires, they sang and told tales,
And finished their evenings, with toast and brown ales.
From Monday to Friday, they worked with a will,
There's lots of folk wish, they were here with us still.
I have lived in Kent, for sixty odd years,
Watched the hop pickers go, with many fears.
The garden of England, has changed such a lot,
I don't think folk realised, just what they'd got.
It's now gone forever and time marches on,
The people the hop fields, have nearly all gone,
They came through the war years, peace-time as well,
And picked all the hops, although the bombs fell.
The Battle of Britain was fought overhead,
They just carried on, 'twas the way they were bred.
These people from London and farther away,
They came down here, for their holiday.
I wish with my heart, that these days would come back,
But, hop picking machines came, they were given the sack.

James Baker

MUSINGS OF A WOODWOSE

If trees were made of plastic
Woodpeckers would be fazed
They'd try to excavate their nests
And get completely dazed
And plastic is so slippery
Bird life could be erased.

If trees were made of iron
We'd have our work cut out
Whenever we were pruning them
Or carting twigs about
And lumberjacks in Canada
Would strike, without a doubt.

If trees were made by glaziers
And we sat on the grass
In autumn time, we'd be beset
By showers of falling glass
Which would be very painful
If the worst should come to pass.

I'm glad that trees are made of wood
And leaves are made of . . . leaf
A tree of gold would be a great
Temptation to a thief
(And nowhere near as beautiful;
At least, that's my belief).

Rosemary Whittingham

'TIS THESE I LOVE

'Twas asked of me what makes you love
Amidst this world so filled with hate
Is it the splendid gifts you have
Those idols unto you relate?
But no 'tis not, please hark a-while
And I will tell you in a trice
As now I speak please do not smile
When finished tender me your sound advice.
These things I love - to walk on grass
Away, away from chimneys grim
And day by day my life to pass
To breathe God's air so free from sin.
Now as my feet on heather tread
'Neath seabirds darkening the sky
I feel warm rain begin to flood
And wonder how we parted you and I.
To be alone 'tis to be alive
I roam this wilderness of man
Existing thus for this we strive
Take now thee gifts of nature's plan.
I pass the hilltop, gaze with awe
Upon the valley under me
'Tis but an artist could paint the score
Of fields and meadows that I see.
The rain has passed, it's finished now
As I walk softly to the waves,
Then let me finish by the shore
'Neath seagulls that pass over me
They say that nature man does move
If true it's then the things I love.

Cyril Saunders

CHILD OF AFRICA

Black as the night, your eyes are the stars
Seeking such penetration from afar,
Your teeth of milk are pearly white
Yet your fading rags reflect your plight.

Child of Africa you seek the meaning
To which abyss is the world then leaning?
Does it wait for Nature's plagues, famines, all
Or await atomic destruction, or simply stall?

As you clasp your empty stomach round
What solace in hollow words have you then found?
Child of Africa with sockets a brilliant red,
Red of defiance or are you now dead?

Waiting on your meagre portion generous given
Would you be better then to wait in Heaven?
As the dust swirls around your shrunken feet
Why will you not our noble leaders greet?

As your teeth drop and so do fall
Your throat so dry, too dry to call
Must you still wait? And still they stall.
Child of Africa you fade from sight
Child of Africa, what was your plight?

Your sockets bare and bones so brittle
The multitudes proven oh so fickle,
Above the telly, the crisps and all
We have ceased to hear your dying call.

Your body melts into the weeping sands
Still grasping at our helping hands.

Mark Lancaster-Purnell

HIGH RISE

This is an awful place to live
Scum is oozing from the paving stones
Litter bins are full to the brim with beer cans
The police do not impound
the cars that are parked illegally
Police hardly come round here

Broken down fences
Houses that haven't seen a lick of paint in years
Damp rot - dry rot - they have it all
Dogs bark - cats litter the streets by the hundred
Nobody seems to own them

The people all have lines on their faces
Time has taken its toll
Living in this neighbourhood does not help

Men gather in the pub for a glass of beer with the usual crowd
Talking of the girls they've had

Spotted youths parading down the street
With spray cans in hand ready to graffiti
the first wall that comes in sight

Lock up your houses - put chains on your door
This is an awful place to live
Scum oozes from the paving stones

Adam R Webb

THE DREADED CV

Why me, why me, who has to fight the world with a CV
Some long, some short, white paper, blue or yellow
Too old at forty, past it now, stale becoming mellow
The years march on, the grey hair starts to show
Depression, anger, resentment sets in, perhaps it's time to go.
Go where? asks my wife.
Whether and why, what are you going to do?
It's like being in a zoo.
Sitting every day so early listening for the postman's steps
Waiting in nervous anticipation and dread
Yes - more rejections of 'No thank you' just fill you with
    terror, it's said.
Forty and past it, no not me!
Oh CV how I've changed you so many times that I now sound
    like Superman not mankind.
This I say to the government, the rest,
My whole life I've worked so hard, fast, been well paid,
    with experience the best
The dreaded CV in all its disguises
So many sent out to date
This man says to you 'Don't forsake me too long before
    it's too late.

Peter S Watson

LITTLE STREAM ON LEITH HILL

Oh! Little stream, babbling and dribbling here unseen,
Now aflame with golden rays from a warm March sun;
This radiant light transforms you, darkest has-been;
Oh! Who will know of your beauty when I am done?

No bard has ever crossed or blessed your existence,
And to a world of ignorance you are unknown;
A place of dark, damp, total insignificance;
All creatures of life your deprived heart would disown.

10

A plot to ignore and find somewhere more adept,
For tourists to clamour, push, prattle, shove or spew,
So alone you remain yet silently accept
This gift of transient beauty befalling you.

And like you, all we need, inside, are golden rays
Of light and truth, grace and love, our Lord sends within,
To reveal lost beauty and rise from dark todays
That bar the growth of man. Quickly let it begin.

Trevor Rowe

UNTITLED

Walk along the Sussex coast
The air will do you good
If you haven't yet ventured here
You know you really should!

There are many places of interest
For young and old alike
Coach trips can be organised
Or the energetic, go by bike!

The Tourist Information Board
Is always close to hand
Or if your wish is to be lazy
You can always lie on the sand.

We have B & B's, camp sites,
Hotels by the score
There are theatres, castles and cinemas
In fact who could ask for more!

If you take the time to visit
You'll see all I've said is true
And maybe then East Sussex
Will be the place for you!

L J Taylor

ALL ALONE

Shivering in the dampness of the cold air,
sitting in a cardboard box, full of despair,
no self respect, feeling used, abused and all alone,
no-one to talk to, no sound of a voice on the phone.

Cannot remember the beautiful sound of a friendly voice,
huddled up, insecure and alone with no choice.
No brothers or sisters to play with and fight,
I just sit here crying day and night.

No family, parents or a friend,
strangers say 'I'll be your friend,' but they only pretend.
Here I stay wet, hungry and cold,
will it be like this all my life, even when I'm old?

All I have is freedom, which some people would cherish,
but this is all I have, and here I'll perish.
What is happiness, when will I eat, how long can I go on?
This is all that fills my mind as the nights grow long.

I realise Christmas is on its way, what will next year bring me?
Perhaps a friendly, familiar face, or just a cold cup of tea.
Being sweet sixteen isn't all that it's cut out to be, I know,
every single day of the year I just feel so low.
I see people pass by, looking at me like dirt,
when they do, deep down I feel so hurt.

Karen Bethell

BIRDSONG

An old man sat on yonder hill
he sat so very, very still.
Scarcely a breath of wind blew past
as his gaze upon the fields he cast;
birdsong lifted his heart and soul
the tears he shed recalled a past parole.
He touched his age, an ancient husk
- refusing spring wanting only a golden dusk,
too tired to stir, he tarried in yesterday
preferring the imperfection of another way.
Quiet, the birds, now they let him rest
sleeping fitfully, he recalls the best
of a world that has left him behind . . .
. . . birdsong resumes as he leaves us resigned,
he is not at all distressed for his spirit senses
the promise of heaven's nest.

S J Beaumont

A DREAM

Was it all a dream?

Were their bodies ever entwined with such passion?

Were those kisses really for her?
Or scattered too easily to be believed?

Were those phrases truly for her?
Or from habit given to another?

About this she chose not to care -
preferring to believe that whilst with her he meant it all.

Julie Thompson

THE LIBERATOR'S SONG

With each mouth the languid liquid transports,
Its warmth and strength imparts the courage for the journey.
Not down highways I must roam,
But down a road less travelled,
That is my memory.
So interned is it, the sepulchre, the recess of my mind.
I fear to unearth those distant hours so long forgotten,
When the elements entwined sang sad lament to fallen men.

We from water came to land on the earth and brave the fire.
Whilst above us Heaven wept a host of men
Each emptied with unwavering intent and with silken web descended.
We men of a mother fought the sons of another.
No white Pegasus on outstretched wings to carry home deliverance.
But sodden khaki, twisted bridge,
And the victorious strains of the lone piper's call.
Surreal fervour grabbed hold, surpassed mortal fear.

Each footprint in the sand, bore testimony to someone's passing.
As waves of Neptune spewed us onto bloody beaches,
All softly shrouded in saline surging,
Rhythmic tidal throb, the pulse of life,
It beat relentlessly.
We prayed it would not stop.
Each erupting thud took with it, into the earth's bowels,
A battle-weary boy, another generation.

Lucifer's tempting could not entice us to a more awful hell,
But so goes the second bar of the Liberator's song,
A mournful wail, the echo of freedom's joy,
This carried always on the grieving lips of mothers,
Who softly touch the sepia image of the Liberator's memory,
And think only that he was too young to die.

Amber Delaney

THE COAST

Fresh and bright is the coast in spring,
In tune with earth's awakening,
Wild grass burgeons in the dunes' rough sand,
Sea birds strut in groups across the strand,
And at the edge of this still sovereign land,
The sea - laps gently.

Summer brings the coming of high sun,
Dazzling our beaches where the children run,
Loving the freedom of their youthful days,
While bathers blister in the heat and haze,
And others sip cool drinks or lie and laze,
And the sea - shimmers.

Autumn - and lamps glow early as night falls,
The shore is bare - we seek our sheltering walls,
Lengthening shadows town and coast enfold
Strange hues streak the sky - purple and gold,
Gather your strength - the year is growing old,
And the sea - murmurs.

Winter descends and now the salt winds chill,
Gales lash the grey-green waters at their will,
Cliffs tower grimly in a shrouding mist,
And like a threatening Evangelist,
Great Neptune stamps his foot and shakes his fist
And the sea - rages.

V Lewis

S'BORO TO 'THE WELLS'

The five-year old knows how to walk
And Grandpapa delights with talk,
As hand in hand they plough their way
On well worn path to reach their prey.
To right of them the calm green fields
To left nought but a holly hedge,
No motor fumes to mar the sun,
Clip clop of horses' hooves alone
To gently soothe the listening one.

What of the prize awaiting them?
'Mount Pleasant' has a pleasing ring,
'Cadena' known throughout with fame.
Little eyes pop quickly out
As through that door she gives a shout:
'Oh Grandpapa meringues I see,
Pure orange juice, what more could be?'

Now, some eighty-six years on
That little girl recalls the scene.
With heart near breaking looks around,
Bricks and mortar left and right,
Polluted air, it could be night,
Simple pleasures don't abound.

Take heed my friends sweet childhood dreams
Lie hidden in this world, it seems.

M Haselden

TIME

Time is a precious gift
that's wasted on the young.
It's only when we're ageing
that we notice just how strong
its influence is.

Days and weeks, months and years
go by
without us realising the ebb and flow.
The tide of Time
gradually eroding all we love and know.

Constantly changing, our world
continues on its course.
Time moulding its shape and form
dramatically, such is its force
and purpose.

And we are but a part of this
continual growth.
We have to learn to bend and sway,
or else we break,
and crumble in dismay.

Time comes around, around, around,
life plays a different tune.
Time past, still not forgotten.
The future yet unknown
and only Time will tell!

Christine Ahern

A ROOM WITH BOOKS

There's feeling in a room with books, the love,
The depth, the warmth of something that's alive.
The ranks and rows of old campaigners stand -
Passed from hand to hand, friend to friend, to me.
The flames in shadow dance upon them all,
Who themselves once danced upon this earth;
Burns, Belloc, Blunden, Bridges, Beardsley, Brooke;
Inscribed with care from lover; mother; friend
Hughes, Hardy, Henley, Hopkins, Hugo, Hood;
In faded hand 'December 1910'.
Books from libraries of Laureates,
Volumes revered as Bibles at the front,
Diaries of dear dead days, letters of love,
Classics, passions, open wounds, injustice.
As full-bodied wine, verse, chapter, stanza,
Spill and flow out across the floodlit lawns,
From leathered desk to some dark, secret place,
And here I sit, surrounded by my friends,
Their words remain though they themselves are gone.
Their lives re-lived within my favourite room.

Mike Read

WAKEHURST PLACE

Wakehurst which suffered from the hurricane
Impressive gardens - closely linked to Kew
Is back again in all its former glory
And once again attractive to the view

Set in the countryside amid the splendour
Of flowers and every other living thing
A place to visit and enjoy in sharing
The lovely freshness of an English spring

The house - which complements the local landscape
Windows reflecting softly-coloured dawns
Rare-timbered slopes - with banks of shrubs enclosing
Wide grassland - gently merging into lawns

If you would wish to spend a quiet moment
What better place is there to choose but here
Released from all the stress of modern living
In such a spot - whose beauty I hold dear

L T Coleman

EARTH-CALL

A patch of land, once tamed, now running wild,
Lies by the wood-yard, near the railway line.
The concrete factories churn out their wares
And, overhead, the power cables whine.

Among the bits of cars and plastic bags,
The flowers fight each year to bloom again,
And little snails with stripy humbug shells
Creep out along the pathways after rain.

A ragged mattress spews its stuffing out,
And gleeful children kick it everywhere;
Yet butterflies still mate above the grass,
And drifts of clover scent the evening air.

Stand quiet there, ears closed to man-made noise,
And listen with your heart; then you will hear,
From every leaf and twig and struggling flower,
The song of undefeated *earth* ring clear.

Anne Chance

WORDS

Bitter words of anger,
Spoken in haste,
Are as a summer storm,
They are of no moment.
Words chosen with care,
And spoken with love, however,
Build one upon the other
Giving a strong foundation
For us to build our lives upon.
Then, in the fullness of time,
We, in turn, pass them onto
            future generations
For their strength and support.

Frances Adams

I'LL FIND MY WAY AMONG THE STARS

I'll find my way among the stars
Walk not to me but away from me
For I must go alone
Remember me as I was
As I remember you
Forever young
Do not grieve long for me
For I have found my way
As you must now find yours
Be not afraid to love again
I know you will find it hard
Fear not that you will be deserting me
For I know you never would
And when at last your time draws near
You will find me here among the stars as I await you dear.

Allison Bishop

20

OH BEXHILL

Oh Bexhill charming Sussex haven
How you remind me of times past
Of quieter days and courteous people
With Edwardian houses designed to last

A promenade to stroll at leisure
Whilst gentle waves caress the shore
With sailing boats of many colours
Who on earth could ask for more?

Ronald F Hall

SPRING

The mud is drying up at last,
The grass is growing now quite fast,
The cows will soon be in the field
With hoped-for rises in their yield
Of milk to put into the tank,
Which means more money for the bank.
The cuckoo soon will come along,
Then we shall hear his joyful song.
The leaves appear upon the trees
And then the humming of the bees
Will fill the air most pleasantly,
Making it a joy to be
Upon a farm when it is spring,
When flowers are here and birds will sing
And build their nests and hatch their eggs.
The lambs will skip and throw their legs
High in the air, so full of play,
But when the grass is cut for hay
It usually begins to rain,
And so the mud comes back again.

W J Saunders

KNOWING

If I were upon the stair and heard footsteps would
      they be yours?
And if you were to reach out for me from the dark
      would you need just cause?
I already know the answer.

Do I have to ask whether the smile within your eyes
      is because of me?
And do you ponder whether this is really where you
      want to be?
I have no doubts.

Can I find comfort in knowing I may always confide
      in the silence of your bed?
And can you have the strength to respect the solitude
      within my head?
I do not need to ask.

Have I the faith to trust in your desire to stay?
And have you the patience to watch as I struggle to
      find my way?
I don't think so
I know.

Karen Tasker

GRANDAD

He limped outdoors and sat on the seat
Grandad I said 'Where's the shoes for your feet.'
He blushed like a child caught in the act
'Worn out!' He muttered 'and so is my hat.'
'Poor Grandad' I said telling my mother
'Tell him,' she replied 'to pull the other.'
'He forgot to put them on' she said
'Remind him now it's time for bed.'

Audrey Park

WINTER HOLIDAY

A winter holiday by the sea
When the crowds have gone and the sands are free
Then I am free to walk where I will
With the wheeling seagulls shrieking shrill
Over grey-green billows out in the bay,
And there's salt on my lips from the wind-blown spray.
There's driftwood then to collect for the fire
As the gale blows strong and the waves beat higher
And I battle my way 'gainst the storm to get back
To tea and toast in our holiday shack.
Yes, a winter holiday, that's for me,
A winter holiday by the sea.

Elizabeth Allday

NIGHTMARE

There was a cry for help
From deepest slumber
Only a dream. I turned away
Unclasping the hands
That begged me to stay.

There was a cry for help
In the midnight shadows
Nothing there - hide in sleep
Ears shut out the demons
Cursing, echoing deep.

There was a cry for help
'The beast devours me!'
I come my child! Fly the stair!
Echoing screams vibrate within me
Door gapes wide - no-one is there!

Patricia Battell

23

CLOUDWALKING

One bright cold morning in December
Chill and cheerful as I remember
The snow near melted on the grass
I stood dawn dreaming of the year gone past.

One year older, hopefully wiser
But who can tell you might be wiser!
A lot can happen spring to winter
A new-built fence that starts with a splinter.

Life and death in the blink of an eye
A razor-edge balance on the question why?
Is life someone's game or an unopened gift?
Or a random selection in an open-air lift?

My mind takes me higher, through yesterday's mist
To an aerial view of things I may have missed
Exams being passed, a race - coming last
A death on the road, a driver too fast.

A walk in the park, the sun on my back
Like a trip in the clouds to heaven and back
A smile from a girl, a baby's new curl
A wish on the wind to bring a good luck pearl.

Neil Gould

MY PARENTS' RUBY ANNIVERSARY

Jesus was smiling up above,
the day he blessed you with His love.
Forty years ago today
memories to always stay.

A happy smile
a silent tear,
One for every passing year.

As the years start to unfold
Seven children to love and to hold.
A place in our hearts we hold on to dear
because without you both, we wouldn't be here.

So much to hope and dreams to forefill
if only time could stand still.
Sixteen grandchildren, you've come a long way
from forty years including today.

P A Ripley

BUTLERS GREEN

Nearing now the house, the halfway landmark
On the way back home.
This house, always seen, always passed,
Stands grey, gaunt, foursquare,
A visual echo of such empty autumn evenings.
Hollow windows stare out unseeing
Like a vacant witness.
Soon level, and walking past, when in the movement of
A moment a quick glimpsed figure takes sudden shape.
From the gate? From the ground? From where? For real?
A trick of the mist.
Yet still a sense that something passed, and
Seemed certainly there, arms outflung in blind flight,
Moving slowly yet passing fast across the road,
Then soon absorbed on the other side
By the long since infilled pond.
This grey spinster vision, which some have seen, appears like this
Then silently dissolves in the chill, still grass
And the damp encroaching dusk.
An out-of-body memory, in seconds out of sight,
Is left behind, passed by in time; but seen, remains in mind.

Cyndy Manton

ODE TO THE SELF-EMPLOYED

They ask how it's going, you say very well
Though you know deep down that it's *bloody hell,*
With business not what you thought it would be
With those creditors threatening bankruptcy,
And the landlord pushing hard for his rent,
How little he knows that it's already spent
On luxuries like food and clothes for the kid
As today you drive at tomorrow, to skid
On unforeseen ice that formed in the night
When everything seemed to be going alright,
Till that dreaded postman turns down the drive,
Or a day's reprieve lending strength to survive.

It would take an army of men such as Freud
To unravel the minds of the self-employed
With the anguish and the apprehension
The cogs of strain enmeshed with tension,
Chasing the accountant every minute
Wondering whether he's dropped you in it,
Fearing lest the bailiffs swarm -
No limited company did you form;
Be sick never nor seek the dole
For that is playing a devious role,
Dispensing with pride in the guise of maturity
Down on your knees at the Social Security.

Things are, of course, not always so grim
When the dog-paddling ceases and you learn how to swim,
Providing the wife can retain her sanity
And the bank still treats you with humanity,
As the scraps are whipped up with expenses all paid,
You can breathe with the breath you alone have made.

Ivor Vernon Smith

DAFFODILS IN THE SNOW

I saw a funny sight today,
as I drove to my work
for on the ground, snow did lay,
the weather's gone berserk.

I thought the time of year was spring,
it is April month, you know.
But this year all it's managed to bring,
is daffodils in the snow.

It started off a lovely day,
with a colourful blossoming show
but as the sun failed to stay,
down came a flurry of snow.

The weather is appalling
how can anything grow
while large flakes keep falling,
presenting daffodils in the snow?

Spring flowers, like to toss their heads
in a lively, sprightly dance,
but now they lay frozen in their beds
and growth hasn't got a chance.

I've never seen such madness
when the North wind did blow,
for have you ever seen such sadness
as daffodils in the snow?

Jackie Figg

A RAIN FOREST CRIES

A rain forest cries
And I cry with it
A storm of sadness.
Emerald light
Exudes from the sky
Your emotions I share,
Please heal the despair
Caressed by the gentle touch
Of leaves against my bare skin,
A great release,
A dam of craziness bursts,
Like a scream into silence
Like oxygen after strangulation
The tornado in my brain
Is released slowly
With every ragged breath I draw
Fighting to control the panic
Darkness for a while overcomes
The torment for any space of time
I sink into the release
I fall through the floor,
And as soon as it started
Reality takes hold.
My contract with sanity is broken
I hold on to my wish
To not just fade away.

Sarah Scantlebury

BARELY TWO

When war came he was barely two
But it swept away the world he knew.
Two years' old, but still enough to plant the seed
Which coloured thought and moulded deed.

Victorian values still held sway
And he kneeled to God on every day.
Nursery rhymes and bombs - courage in despair -
As brave men died leaving contrails in the air.

Father in khaki; a stranger now.
And a distant mother with troubled brow.
But still he says his prayers; learns gentle things.
Holding hope on solid silver wings.

At seven the bloody thing is done
And victory that cost too much is won.
Still old values - simple joys enjoyed.
Little wealth but everyone employed.

Boarding school is quite pre-war,
Ruled by stern paternal law.
Rugger, cricket, rationing. And soon he knew:
'The game is more than the player,
And the ship is more than the crew.'

P A Tolhurst

AFRAID FOR THE FUTURE

Stop, think, look around and see,
The thought of our world now terrifies me,
Death through hunger, war and pain,
It's happening everywhere again and again,
Children being murdered, untold shedding of blood,
Lives destroyed by bombs, famine or flood,
Crime is on the rampage, we can't stop it now,
The reason isn't simple, we just don't know how,
Sleeping on concrete, surviving through drugs,
Young men who are angry are turned into thugs,
People of all kinds thrown into the mix,
Not knowing where they're going, what'll be their next fix,
Violence and perversion, we're afraid for our lives,
Waiting for the moment we're confronted with knives,
Innocent people dying, the guilty roam free,
I am scared and I am tired, do you feel like me?
Politics and power, money and greed,
Where are we heading, just where will it lead?
Dominating all animals to prove we are strong,
Expendable creatures, I'm sure this is wrong,
We are suffocating our planet, sentencing it to death,
How long can it manage with only one breath?
We are the reason why this Earth turns,
Don't you think it's time the *human race* learns?

Nikki Terry

SOUNDS AND SIGHTS I LOVE

Blackbird there upon the post,
Songs like yours I love the most,
Birds and flowers, all of these,
And the music in the trees.
There is movement in the sky,
When the wind is rushing by,
There is rhythm in the earth,
When the spring is giving birth,
There are birdsongs on the hill,
In the summer evening still.

Windmills white, gentle breeze,
Dreamy downs, buzzing bees,
Craggy cliffs, proud and high,
Fields so green, sapphire sky,
Crying, gliding gulls in flight,
Dusk falls, then creatures of the night,
Once more the mystery trails pursue,
'Til later, breaks the dawning new!

Vera Way

THE LAST GOODBYE

Lay your hand on a fevered brow,
Time is passing quickly now.
Let your eyes your love express
No need for words or last regrets.
Embrace their heart for just awhile
And your reward, a lasting smile.
Sit silently and you will hear
Peace and love so close and near.
We never part just go away
Until we meet again one day.

Enid Deeprose

WHEELS

Auto racing over wild terrain
Wipers clicking in the rattling rain
Speedo moving up to ninety-two
Till a sudden splash of cobalt blue
Lightens up the sodden Nordic sky
And the wetness is transformed to dry.
Next an empty desert highway
With Sinatra singing 'My Way'.
Car and driver coming to a stand
Before a canyon, pink and mega grand.
Silence. . . . car and driver pose.
Then in some mid-Atlantic prose
A disembodied voice
Explains the happy choice
That you and I will make
With this super-turbo-diesel brake.
GL, GT this, XJ, GD that.
An alphabet of tittle-tat.
A blast of Mahler! Off again
To the city on the centre lane
And not another car in sight.
Is there anyone on earth who might
Be that silly, be that mad
To believe this splendid ad?

Elizabeth Clifford

AN OIL SPILLAGE

Another disaster, another spoil,
A natural wilderness
Tarnished by oil.

A black slick stretches
Both far and wide.
Coating the beaches
Brought in by the tide.

Unsuspecting birds
Dive into the sea of death.
Seals and fish die
Gasping for breath.

We see the misery
Suffering and pain.
But can we ever stop this scene of horror
From happening again?

Gordon H Butchers

PARTNER, FRIEND

Straight and true was the furrow you drew,
The ploughman's pride as the trail you trod:
Breaking new ground, bearded Cortés astride,
Montezuma saw, in awe, as a god.

Across the steppes your forebears poured,
Mongol flags unfurled,
Their thunder in the Golden Horde
Terrified the world.

Copenhagen at Waterloo, held
Wellington amidst men's dreadful screams;
The Emperor's pale Marengo, who
Shared sad Napoleon's shattered dreams

A horse; dog meat! A course for man,
A treat, delicacy? Forfend!
Better a partner, friend to us,
A legacy from Pegasus

Who from Medusa's death-blood sprang,
Curbed Helicon's Mount, with a kick, to bring
Divine inspiration, the Hippocrene Spring,
Aesthetic sense to the mind of *man*.

Sydney Oates

A SPRING WALK

A spur of the moment decision,
Made on a wonderful sunny day,
That I shall follow the floating clouds,
As my guide to show me the way.

A short walk through happy streets,
Where families are playing together,
Then up and over a stile,
Onto paths of infinite measure.

A slow and glittering stream,
Is the first thing that I see,
Resting among banks of flowers,
Being tended by a lazy bee.

And then onwards and further,
Along the steady paths I know,
Occasionally meeting happy people,
Wishing me good health as I go.

It seems not far into my walk,
That I hear a faint rushing sound close by,
I pause to listen for a second,
To rest under the shining sky.

And so, not far away,
The reward of my journey is found,
A peaceful, small lake ripples in the sun,
With laughing water all around.

I sit down for a while to think,
And watch a swan slowly gliding past,
I know I have found true happiness,
Here, in my heart, at last.

Rachel Lindfield

ALONG THE DOWNS

Along the downs
On a still autumn day
Some gentle soul had breathed
So lightly, so sweetly
Touching the rise and fall
Of grassy steeps
With a whisper of blue haze.
And warmth of summer
Over late
Lulled the ancient hills
Into a strange glory.
Wrapped in beauty
So serene
Had no need
Of my adoration
My devotion.
And loneliness
Stirred my senses
And other loves
Forgotten in tranquillity
Blazed into intensity
And ecstasy
And longing and pain
Ever remain.
And the ageless Downs
So loved
Lie passionless
To the beating
Of my yearning heart.

Eileen Symes

THE UNSPOKEN DEED, IS ON OUR STREETS . . .

I put pen to paper yet again . . .
To thank you for your response in vain.
An ugly fracas two days this week,
Of how this unfeeling tax may speak.

Both Peter and you reply,
And I with a heavy sigh . . .
Within this paper logged by both,
It does not help to mend the wrath.

Too much is gained by the spouse who cares,
This monetary system to bare.
The way, the will of the officers . . .
They do not care, they want their coffers . . .

The unspoken deed, is on our streets,
Suicides lay upon the floor at our feet.
It's no good to prepare such proof,
The words just leaving one aloof . . .

The wasted time and value, I care,
I hope my words you find value there.
To go out and speak about this unfair tax,
Of which a review, and to axe.

Do not be disheartened by my words,
This is proof that they have been heard . . .
Just think that when another divorcee calls,
That what I say is not a load of balls!

Ann Hubbard

THE MARLBOROUGH HOTEL - ST LEONARDS ON SEA

Ever gaunt, in shadow, the Marlborough portal, darkly, glowers,
Across worn steps and balustrades with etched, heraldic flowers.
Whispers from a bygone age, curl in dancing disarray,
Partnered, in the swirling dust, by long lost dreams of yesterday.
Shattered windows, blindly bare, sightless to the scene before,
Majestic brows of architraving, an epitome the very core
Of man's endeavour to construct a vision of perfection,
Stark, rotting teeth - cracked chimney pots, having no protection
From nature's wrath, the roaring winds and salted sprays,
Whipped across the white caps - from Siberian, frozen wastes.

Ghostly airs of Big Band music, chandeliers of crystal light,
Echoes of an entertainment, gone - for ever, overnight.
Wheeling, shrieking heron gulls alight on twisted tortured eaves,
A busy spider contemplates the flies caught in the web she weaves.
Glimpse of ballroom, parquet floor, dulled mosaic centre piece.
Yellowed, crumbling plaster cherubs - nose-less, ear-less ceiling frieze.
Turrets tower, tersely grave, over the silent park band stand,
Where once the favoured few played to the many privileged grand.
Scent of roses gently wafts through wrought-iron balconies, fused
By rust and time - Victoria turns her back distinctly not amused.

Morose, debauched, The Marlborough stands tall with fragile pride,
Her solid walls reverberate with the sounds of years gone by.
The Hotel sign and crowns - symbols of her comfort worth,
Hang broken flapping hollowly against her massive girth.
Each sitting Council's party piece, subject of so many plans,
Shelved, rejected, frayed by protecting conservation bans.
Modern voices of St Leonards link with ancient, anxious frowns,
Protesting with a growing clamour against the pulling down
Of such a monument - eternal beauty underneath decay,
Overwhelming heritage value must live to serve another day.

Christine Baxter

LET THE WHITE DOVE FLY AGAIN

Come on my lads, and over the top,
these words their Officers cried.
Then over the top in their thousands went
and in fields of mud, they died.

Those fine young men of tender years
so proud were they to go.
And fight for their King and Country
against a raging foe.

They didn't ask for reasons
like how, or where and why.
But gladly they marched off to war
as their loved ones waved goodbye.

But why do these conflicts happen
are young men doomed from birth?
To fight and die in a foreign land
and for what, a few feet of earth.

Now our leaders should all be united
and make sure, that all wars must cease.
So that sons and daughters can live normally
and our grandchildren grow up in peace.

And if humans could now make an effort
to end all this misery and pain.
Then live together in close harmony
and let the white dove fly again.

R H Turke

WAR CRIMES

Understanding is an instinct
From which we run away,
Confronting all the big issues
To keep the truth at bay.
Our destinies are interlinked
But war we'd rather wage,
Accumulating scar tissue
Which helps to fuel the rage!

Where does pride stop - and vanity begin
When did all our values get revised?
How can we continue in iniquity and sin
With bigotry and hatred on the rise?

The memory can sometimes be
The worst friend that we've got
I've seen into the soul of thee
And learned what you've forgot.

Through twists and turns and fragrant words
We people live a lie
My love is tested daily
But without it, where am I?

A place akin to limbo
Where the truth can never reign
A staggering crescendo
Of war cries creating pain;

Are borders more important
Than the people they contain?
Have you been blinded by the vision
Of the hopelessly insane?

Damien Hoadley-Brown

TO KENT - GREETINGS

My greeting to you, O my Kent, O my county,
How often my feet on your byways have strayed!
For how many years have you given of your bounty
When in your dominion in boyhood I played?

How often, how often my vision has captured
A thrill in the glory of yon setting sun!
How often, at even, my soul was enraptured
By stars set a-twinkling e'er night had begun.

And still are your woodlands as wild and beguiling,
Your pastures as pleasant, your fields still as fair.
With winter's dark frowning or summer's bright smiling
Your hills are resplendent, if greenclothed or bare.

But of your free rivers the Medway is flowing
Majestic and splendid in full stately tide.
And Rochester's castle still grimly is showing
To city behind and the river beside.

Augustine and Gundulf and Lanfranc have stayed here,
And set up their altars where darkness had dwelt.
The saint and the penitent often have prayed here,
Before the High Altar where thousands have knelt.

But still I may walk where your country delights me
And still I may gaze at the scene spread afar!
The years may pass by, but your beauty requites me,
Before I fly upward to Time's Evening star.

H E Hoadley

WATCHING IT HAPPEN

Two soaring sentinels
gently swaying
safe harbour,
for siskin, bluetit
thrush.
Their lime greens
pierce blue skies
in autumn's misty sun.

A truck, three men
survey their height
a buzz saw,
a long arm
reaches up
to pull the trees apart.
Branch by branch
they flop to the ground
waving wildly
their last farewell.

Two naked houses
left behind
harbouring humans,
Gone forever,
birds and beauty.

Daphne A Baker

SADNESS

We're glad to have our loved ones here
Around us every day.
We like to feel that they are near
And not to go away.

Now we all know that life must end
As death is very sure.
We lose a dear one or a friend
For grief - we find no cure.

It was last year I felt this pain
Because my Grandma died.
And now I'll not see her again
Oh, how I cried and cried.

I loved her lots and she loved me,
To visit her was fun.
Her kindness to her family
Was seen by everyone.

I'd like to talk to her and say
What I've achieved this year.
Oh will my sadness go away?
I wish she still was here.

E H Turner

THE CHURCHYARD

We sat there God and I in the graveyard, silent and serene,
Pockets full of dead, some with stone crosses at their head.
All facing east, some with flowers some with weeds,
Angels, headstone, vases, urns, I wonder when will it be my turn?
I said, 'God why do we die? Leaving our loved ones left to cry'
God said, 'You are only passing through make sure there's good in all
you do.'

'I will call when I see fit, I call some early, call some late.
But all will reach that golden gate.'
I created a world for all to share,
But now it's animosity and greed.
Some call it progress, some say hate,
Some are rich, so many in need.
So sit awhile, enjoy my world before it is too late.
Just sit here with me, and we will contemplate.

Patricia Farmer

PERFIDIA

The coldness of your eyes belongs to the wind,
A bitter blast
Blows the fragments of faded friendship
Gently to earth,
Crushed by your thoughtless footsteps.

A memory seals my lips forever,
A quenched candle
Reveals the darkness of deceit
Suspended in silence,
Exposed by your whispered treachery.

The scar you inflicted will never be sealed,
My pale pity
Searches for the spirit of salvation
Drowning in distrust,
Created by your callous cruelty.

Listen,
The echo of my laughter in the hollow of your heart.

Rebecca Pearse

PERFECT BLUE

For what it's worth
I dedicate this day to us.
The glorious sunlight becomes you
And dances in your eyes with a brilliant light
That renews the emotion -
It is so warm here in our love.
Surrender your body to the day
Remember how languid you can feel
Think back to the aftermath of passion.
So soft and calm is the very air
That it kills the echo of past sorrow
And makes us timeless, untouchable.
Our lives may move with the clouds
But today is still, is perfect blue
The colour of momentary joy.

Sharon Tyson

NAN

You stole from me my oldest friend
and put a stranger in her place.
My great old-fashioned parent
You've stripped her of her grace.

You crumble all her wisdom,
and make her lose her way.
You take away her mind
but you let her body stay.

Can't find a way to reach her,
or find comfort for her tears.
What kind of justice is it
that robs her of her years?

Helen Sellers

GRIEF

Thirty years - so many tear drenched years
Of mourning and wanting you.
Longing to feel you touch my hand,
Your strong arm guiding me along life's way.
Enfolding me in contented happiness,
A warmth of love, not of this world.
The sun shines brightly, but its rays are cold.
Stars shine in midnight heaven, but no story told.
Of intense enduring love, burning through time,
Waiting to be united in the cold grave's depth.
The rainbow hues of earth's fair flowers.
Bloom briefly and are gone, bringing no joy in their sweetness.
But still I bring them to your grave.
To heal the soreness of my heart,
And when at last my time is done,
If it be God's will, my soul unites with yours.
Then we will know true happiness once more,
For all eternity.

J Middleton

LANDSCAPE OF LIFE

The landscape sets the seen of life,
Without it, beauty cannot be,
An artist's impression is not shown,
Without a landscape of quality.

Its image of either dark or light,
Can mean one of joy or distress,
But whatever the scene or setting,
It is life above the rest.

Ian Short

THIS ENGLAND

Oh my England, what have we done,
Lost are the wild places one by one.
Gone are the hedgerows ripped and torn
The marshes drained and all forlorn.
Tear it out and cut it down
Destroy it for the mighty pound.
Money is the god you see
Important more than deer or tree.
Who raise their eyes the sky to see
Foul gases up there floating free.
You cannot hear the country sounds
Aeroplane the whole lot drowns.
Rivers foul with fish all dead
Birds cannot find their daily bread.
In cities human termites live
To prey on old and take not give.
Oh England love, what have we done
Would it were we'd just begun?

Ron Surman

THE BEACH

As we galloped through the
sea, water sprayed up behind
flying hooves.

His chestnut coat gleamed in
the sun as we jumped the
rolling waves.

His silky mane waved
in the wind
As the hoofprints in the
sand gradually disappeared.

Hayley Elliott (12)

IN PRAISE OF MOTHER THERESA

All women are proud of you
The highest honours are your due.
Although your health is frail
You do not fail.
To continue good deeds -
To sow further seeds -
To dedicate, encourage, inspire
To follow fire with fire.
Yours is a life beyond compare
Of devotion and selfless care.
We pray that at some future date
You will enter into the Heavenly gate -
As Saint Theresa.

Olive Gray

THE MISER

Some people will tell you, money is bad
But I'm afraid that I cannot agree.
For I've kept all the pennies that I ever had,
They're collectable items you see.

And I can't see the sense, in buying new gear
It's a complete waste of money I say.
For I want my cash, right close by and near
In my hands at the end of each day.

But you can't take it with you, or so it's been said
Now that would bring tears to my eye,
For they tell me you cannot keep it when dead
But I intend to have a good try.

B Went

DEEP IN THE NIGHT

Deep in the night, time it moves so very slowly,
waiting for the safety of morning, silence surrounds you.
Your thoughts and emotions engulf you
each second in the darkness you fight to endure.
Desperately trying not to drown in your mind's turmoil,
finally you manage to escape, to sleep.
Yet it follows you into your dreams
you find yourself running, looking for a place to hide.
Hoping you'll find the light
and with it the blissful peace your soul is yearning for.
Suddenly the dream stops
waking to find the sunlight of morning.
Still the night it haunts you
lying in the warmth of the sun.
Watching the clouds gliding through the sky
seeking the peace only nature can provide.
Your mind floating outside your body, the soul it soars
experiencing the beauty and wonder of the world.
Realising how very small a part you are in the history of mankind
and even smaller in nature's infinite cycle.
Returning to the body refreshed
the solutions seem so clear, so easy.
Life's pressures float away on the breeze
the answer so simple all children know it.

Grace Dacruz

AUTUMN

The autumn scene is wondrous to behold
With falling leaves of yellow, red or gold
A blood red sun sinks in a sombre sky
The wind rustles through the trees with a sigh
Over all there is an air of peace
As nature prepares for its winter sleep.

J Neal

CONFESSIONS

Although I am a happy wife
there is something I must confess.
I have two other men in my life
do I love them too 'oh yes'!
I see them as often as I can
and we always kiss and hold hands.
Sometimes we go for a walk in the park
being with them is really just grand.
Now all this is not really a problem
as I am sure you now will see.
I like to be with my grandsons
and they like to be with me!

Anita Steadman

LAST NIGHT OF OCTOBER

Oh, how the baring branches stare and sigh,
At the moon's glow, at the moon's cold, boated light,
And point their jagged fingers up,
And dance and dance on this fair October night.

Look! How the fragile Abbey's spires and towers
Linger in shadow, rise at last to shine,
And smile and shimmer in the moon's cold light;
These are the grapes for sweet October wine.

But now my hurrying feet run faster yet,
Down empty streets, on moonlit patterned stone,
To find each shadow the contour of your face,
To flee from you this lovely light night, alone.

But how you are with me! How above in trees
Your voice echoes, lingering in the choirs
Of falling leaves, stones and human hearts
And all things waiting for November fires.

Joy Ottewill

POVERTY

Everywhere you look around
Homeless feet they stray.
Just victims of the 3rd world
Almost dead they lay.

Emotions swirling in the mind
A debate you might well say,
Of glancing back at the homeless
Almost dead they lay.

To you the sight is blinding
But others brush them away.
With no home to go to
Almost dead they lay.

To them it's just another bomb
That drops along the way.
But as the smoke drifts upwards
Almost dead they lay.

Samantha Bosworth (11)

POISON

And I wish that you could love me
In a way that I could touch,
And I dream that I could hold you
In a time that doesn't stop.
I long for you to want me,
Like a drug you can't afford,
I'd die for you to kiss me,
Like a poison for my thoughts.

Emma Whiteman

LIFE

Life is like a classic drama
The world a mighty stage.
Everyone a member of the cast
No matter what their age.

So from tragedy to comedy
The pattern often ranging.
For in this everlasting saga
The scenes are ever changing.

Everyone will play a part
However large or small.
Until the grand finale
Till that last curtain call.

When that last act is done
And that final curtain falls.
Our acting days are over,
When the great Producer calls.

L P Bennett

SUSSEX

From the smoke of London I came,
Riding in front of the van, bringing my home with me.
Ever do I remember seeing the sign East Sussex
Rolling hills, green pastures, sheep and trees
A different life, with new friends, new interests
And for me enjoying all.

This is Sussex, small towns, lovely villages, primroses and violets
And Sussex by the sea.

Betty Nash

LADY AT LEYSDOWN

I love you
Lady on the beach.
Watching the waves
Touching your feet.
And the sun draping
Its afternoon on your shoulders.
A yellow light
Across the pale white there.

I love you
My lady on the sand,
Hearing yours hands'
Quiet conversation.
Listening to what lips say
Only breathing,
And to what your breath says
Only lisping.

I love you
O my lady of the hour.
Your fingers finding time
For me,
Your mouth's discovery
Of my somehow good,
My sometime grace.
My something like enchantment
At what most
Is like
Your love.

Kevin O'Keeffe

PRELUDE

Not the years so much, but
The miles have chipped away
At him. If he could just be still -

Now, just arrived. Standing at the
Kitchen door, still breathing smoke and
Tired, he wears the journey's lonely

Thoughts around his eyes. Not smaller
But somehow less significant.
I notice more grey hairs in his

Moustache. His tight, strong calves over
Exmoor hills had carried us, through
Heather and gorse. Then, I saw flecks

Of fleece on the barbed wire fence; questioned
The sheep's cumulous sacrifice.
Does it hurt them? Tell me. Does it?

He won't stop for a cup of tea.
Saying 'Come on, son, get your things'
With a tense jingle of car keys.

Driving. Searching for a time to ask.
'I don't know, son, I just don't know,'
Flicking ash from the open window:

Hot cinders. A moment of amber
In the night. Quickly forgotten
And left behind. I hear the car's

Traffic lost diminuendo -
My tears are only half my own;
But all my own the welcome back.

Jacob Townsend

THE DAY OUT

Do you remember that day on the pier?
You had a cornet and I had a beer.
Watching the seagulls screaming in flocks
Dropping their messages, daubing our frocks.
Dashing for shelter out of the rain
(If you want sunshine, get off to Spain!)
Do'nuts and pizzas, packets of crisps,
Hamburgers, Cola, chicken and chips.
Bingo and scratch cards, yes, it's all here!
Takes all your money, a day on the pier!
Trips on the briny four times a day,
Choose between Sally or Dorothy May.
Bobbing and rocking we're leaving the shore,
'Hold tight m'darling! Room for one more.'
Snoring in deckchairs, sun-hats askew,
Time for a cuppa', a bun and the loo.
Quick! There's the coach and they're ready to go,
Can't you run faster? Don't be so slow.
We've had a good day down on the pier,
Cheerio Brighton!
See you next year!

Gwenda Stanton

ISLAND SUNRISE

Early morning island sunrise
Blue ocean paradise.
Easter Island in the moonglow
People dancing singing low.

By the water Holy Water
Ocean bathed little daughter.
How the people raised her high
Little children learn to fly!

Early morning, Easter Island
How the statues understand.
About the sun and the stars
And the moon above so far.

Easter morning sing in tune
To the waxing waning moon.
Feel the dawning of the sun
New re-birth for everyone.

Avelin

TO JIM

Remember when long ago,
You smiled and said, 'I love you so'
I remember, you were forty-three
And meant all the world to me.
Remember when you gave me a ring
Big and shiny, such a splendid thing.
Sapphires for love, Opals for hope
How could I have been such a silly old dope?
All those years spent waiting and wailing,
Expecting life to be all plain sailing.
Our engagement now is fourteen years long,
And our hair turned to silver just like the song.
You promised a house fit for two,
Then went and bought one just for you.
Life goes on just as it's always done,
Work and work and not much fun.
Why is it others fulfil their dreams
Whilst mine fall apart at the seams?
I'll just close my eyes and recall if I can,
The Jim I first knew, and not this old man.

Hazel Grant

MIND SET

Direction of thought, chaotic revival
Isolating emptiness suffocating survival.
Returning memories thrusting forward,
Intensifying confusion, tumult, disorder.
Panic promoting mental paralysis
Regurgitative processes inducing catharsis.
Inexperienced emotions enduring internalised
Haunting spectres remaining unexorcised.
Shattered mind mechanisms, coping abilities
Hollow perception completing debility.
Abandonment beyond absolute nothingness.
Intuitive faculties totally meaningless.
Judgement concluded, the final analysis
Verdict pronounced. Renewal, synthesis.
Sentence dictates everlasting punishment
Unattainable objective, lifelong imprisonment.

S Tester

BUTTERFLIES

I wandered through a
Cloud of butterflies,
Their wings the colour
Of a rainbow in a silver sky,
Tinged with gold and
Lit by the summer sun.

It is so sad to think
That these delightful creatures
Soon will die,
Fluttering to earth
In death, lost,
Their beauty gone forever.

Teresa Jeanne Smith

MEMORIES - A TRIBUTE

By her cottage fire she sits,
The smoke takes up her dreams.
She's old and tired, peaceful now
And happy so it seems.

She dreams of life so long ago
Long winter days and cold.
As she roamed the lanes and byways
And from her basket she sold.

Her basket was a treasure chest
Aprons, ribbons, laces.
(Quality always the best)
One yard was nose to finger tip
It never failed the test.

It wasn't always winter
She loved the summer times.
When she drove her little pony trap
For many, many miles.
To greet long distant customers,
With their warm and welcoming smiles.

'The Big' houses, she called them
The Manor, The Grange, the Farm.
They'd cross her palm with silver
She never foretold harm.

Her jet black hair has faded now
Dark eyes still brightly shine.
A true blue blooded Romany
This Grandmother of mine.

Yona Geddes

THE BRIGHTEST CANDLE

I have no way of knowing when the darkness came first,
    I had no memory of light that could be proved.
Black despair had swallowed me, but that was not the worst,
    I knew that hell was waiting if I moved;
But help came, as it will, when least expected,
      And flicker though it may,
          The candle that you lit burns in my heart today.

To stand so cold, so sore, so tired, so lonely,
    And hear the evil voices in my nightmare;
Who would know I wept? My tears fell inside only,
    And yet *you* saw it, *you* saw me crying there.
You looked into the darkness, and you found me,
      And flicker though it will,
          The candle that you lit in my heart is burning still.

My legs were scorched by acids from my body's fright,
    My body stank so, even I would choose to move away.
I shook with fear, disgust, despair and madness in the night,
    How *could* you have held me, loved me, brought yourself to stay.
Your warmth enfolded me with light and caring,
      And flicker though it might,
          The candle in my heart is burning just as bright.

And with that little light at last I saw,
    How very close the edge of some awful abyss deep.
You took my hand, and led me from that fascinating door,
    You told me that I had some purpose still to keep.
That other flames would illuminate my soul,
      But flicker though it will,
          The candle that you lit is the brightest candle still.

John Harding

UNHAPPINESS IN ME

Feeling so alone
Afraid and scared in this home.
No-one to talk and be happy with
Why do I feel this way? My head's a sieve.
I feel confused knowing no-one will be around,
To comfort and care for me I must be bound.

Promises and trust are all broken,
Not a single word is spoken.
I feel unwanted as if I shouldn't be here
Why! Oh why! Is there so much I fear?
I keep thinking it over in my head,
Wishing, wondering maybe I should have said,
What a life I have been lonely all the time,
And why can't I stay happy and fine?

I wish you would understand what I feel,
An empty jug not ready to spill.
The sound of happy people and screams,
Just rip me to pieces or split me to the seams.
Why, can't I cheer up, and make the top?
Until I was the highest and couldn't stop
I used to be the happiest person I ever knew.
But now it's gone,
And I know my life is through . . .

Joanna Gayford

MY HOME TOWN

I love to travel out and around
But always pleased to be back on home ground.
The Garden of Eden for good fruit crops,
And of course the best Kentish hops.
Lots of lanes and country roads,
Feathered friends and frogs and toads.
It's not far from London or the sea
But still this place is for me.
A lovely castle with good walking space,
Three old churches and big Grammar School.
Make our town a popular place,
I've lived here from the day I was born,
And love my Kentish town.
So if I go on holiday, I know where my
Seeds are sown.
My town is called Tonbridge in the very
Heart of Kent.
Yes, I'm proud it's my home and that's
Truly meant.

Duggie

MEMORIES

A quiet lane soft edged with grass,
Through which no car could ever pass.
And standing within a garden small,
A country cottage with chimneys tall.

Leaded windows shining bright,
Bathed in the evening's soft sunlight.
And framed in the cottage open door,
The mother whom I will see no more.

With greying hair and faded dress,
She welcomed me with soft caress.
And later in the fire's warm light,
We sat and talked into the night.

Though ne'er more will I hear her voice,
Yet in my heart I can rejoice.
That all the love she gave to me,
Still lives on in my memory.

Audrey Crittenden

SUFFERING APPLE

You say that you have suffered more,
But how do you know what's at the core?
Bite deep within to see the pips
For nothing for sure shall fall from these lips.
The blossom soon to adorn perfect pink with no thorn,
Then to follow rosy red will form.
Once ripe and lush to be plucked,
To be used and crushed, to be pressed to bring forth juice with its zest.
Then still further to be fed upon the ground by the zealous pest.
Now mother tree lay all but bare,
No further blossom to adorn her hair or ensnare.
Stripped down deep to her bark, for now it is all but dead.
But what's that in yonderfield
Is it not a young sapling soon to yield?
The same hue of blossom and rosy red
Does it also have the same sweet taste and allure now fit to shed.
Bite deep once again to the pips.
Can I now tempt you further to speak the unspoken from your lips.
I will ask once more what lays at the core, there is no reply as before,
One thing remains certain, you do not know that's for sure.

K Adams

61

BEARING THE RIGHT THINGS IN MIND

Christmas is coming and the geese are getting fat,
Do you remember times gone past when we used to say that?
Now those days are long since gone and it's no longer funny,
When Christmas comes nowadays, it's money, money, money.
Did we forget to tell our kids what Christmas is really about?
When that little Baby Boy was born, did we forget to shout?
About joy and love and fun and giving,
Surely there must be more to living,
Than work and toil and stress and tears?
Let's turn that clock back through the years,
Remember Jesus born in the stable,
His mother's joy as in her arms she cradled,
The child who one day would grow into the man,
Who would save us from sin.
Do we really understand
The impact this event has on the world today?
Why in the midst of our life we should stop and pray,
So when Christmas time is here this year,
Let's not worry or shed a tear,
For the presents and money we cannot find.
But let us instead bear in mind,
That God sent His Son as sacrifice for our sins.
So let's stop worrying about these silly little things
And on Christmas Eve when Santa comes,
To bring lots of presents from us dads and mums.
Let's not forget how it came about
And never be ashamed to shout
That Jesus was born to save our souls,
And sinning must stop, that's one of our goals.
So now I've come to the end of my ditty,
The truth of which is not too pretty.
Let us promise to tell the story
That 'God' not Santa must take all the glory.

Ann Liles

THE DNA OF SOUND

God spoke *The Word*
But none was there to hear.
He'd started up
The universe we know.

But did *The Word(s)*
Completely disappear
Or does some small part
Thicken the thin air?

Does every crash, scream, whisper
Disappear?
Or does some vital trace
Always remain?

Do all sounds leave a fragment
Out in space?
Which future scientists
Might later trace?

And later reconstruct to bring
The whole sound back
From years ago
Via sonic DNA?

So sometime
From a DNAophone
May people hear
The Holy Voice of God?

James Franks

TREES

In the winter you look so bare
So black and cold you do appear.
Nature has its reasons to treat you so,
It's a resting period as well we know.

A few months, then the buds begin,
Birds bustle in your branches as they sing.
The earth warms up, green leaves appear,
Everything comes to life, spring is here.

Now it's summer - another display,
You've become a shelter, should we pass your way.
So much to offer to birds and beast,
We must appreciate your beauty at the very least.

Autumn colours now in full array,
Nothing can match this wonderful display.
An artist would like to paint this scene,
But only nature has the perfect screen.

So, contractors put our minds at ease,
Please don't keep cutting down our trees.
Stop! Think how much they are giving,
To ensure that we have a healthy living.

Gladys C'Ailceta

MY WILL TO LIVE

O Lord, help me to get out of this bed,
And help me face the day ahead,
All things that would crowd in to crush me,
O Lord, help me to remember where I should be.

(I should be)
Walking at the side of You,
Seeing life with a different view,
Making time for me to pray,
So I can hear all you say,
Making time to read Your Word,
And passing on all I've heard,
So another little lonely soul,
Can turn to You to be made whole.

(I should be)
Remembering all the things you've done,
To make my past a thing dead and gone,
That my life is only half fulfilled,
The best is yet to come still,
I should do all this, and so much more,
Before I enter through Your heavenly door,
So Lord, this is all I can say,
Keep me loving you throughout this day.

And now the evening is finally here,
I've found this day was nothing to fear,
When I was in bed struggling in prayer,
You quietly and lovingly drew near,
Thank You Jesus for all You give,
Your love, Your heart, my will to live.

Debbie McQuiston

THE LONDON EVACUEE

The war had started
It was really bad
We had to go and leave mum and dad.
Oh where are the teachers
Who were good to us then?
All lonely children aged around ten.
I wish I could find them
They could come down to tea
Especially if they have moved to
Sussex like me.
I'd never seen the country
So this would have been a treat,
In fact, I had never been out of the street.
Our school was a hut in the recreation ground,
But it had a good fire and it was sound.
The milk on the fire on a cold winter's day,
Kept us all warm and happy at play.
The village was Washington,
Such a nice place.
The people were kind,
So the hurt was erased.

E R Cuff

SEASONS IN KENT

In leafy lanes between the Downs
Autumn comes to Kentish towns.
Windswept and wet through
One seeks shelter under churchyard yew.

Winter turns the scene to white
And temperatures, minus, grip the night.
Logs from orchards cast aside
Fuel the grates for warmth inside.

But spring in time comes grinning through
An early sign: the morning dew.
Across the fields for maize and corn,
The seasons change and fruits are born.

At last, in full flood, the sun shines down
Throughout the lanes of Kentish town,
Its heat, intense, scores fields anew
And one seeks shelter under churchyard yew.

John A Corney

DANBURY REVISITED IN APRIL 1970

How far into eternity's deep sea
Can I see now, although the tree
Beside the pond, gathers the light
And lights the downward angle
Of the roof, and the pool with spangle
Ripples green and glancing gold
And all that's here is old.
   But here I am adrift upon a thought
   That started many centuries ago,
   And I must keep my little bark afloat,
   Not moving, nor desiring more to know
   Than the tree knows in converse with the sun.
   Perhaps I have been here since days begun,
   Before the roads crossed on this little hill,
   When birds sang and the summer air was still
   And a lone traveller came to sit and rest,
   Under the tree whose gentle shade is blessed.
   Perhaps he knew of me in this far time,
   And I have but to sit and hear the chime
   That sounds in space when past and present meet,
   And Heaven will lie open at my feet.

Marion B Alford

THE DIET

I'm overweight and must forbear,
From lovely things for which I care,
Banished are fried eggs and bacon,
Sausages, mash - all forsaken,
Hidden is the frying pan,
Which cooks the chips and battered spam.
Farewell to all those rich fruit cakes,
The currant buns and chocolate flakes.
No eating out at restaurants fine,
On gourmet food and vintage wine.
Adieu, alas, to claret and port,
They made me such a jovial sort!
Goodbye to all the nuts and cheese,
They made me fat, they make me wheeze.
Gone, forever, the 'glorious binge',
On which so many friendships hinge.
I'm all alone, a social misfit,
With lettuce leaf and water biscuit,
No treats, no hope, no consolation,
To ease despond and desolation.

R K Domin

THE LOVE OF THE SEASONS

To me you're like the seasons of life
Summer being the warmth in your heart
Your warmth makes me feel so good
I can't bear us being apart

Autumn is your colourful personality
Like the changing of the leaves
When you told me I'd stolen your heart
I felt like the richest of thieves

Winter is full of spirit
Bringing happiness to everyone
This is you all over
Love, happiness and fun

Spring, brings change for the better
Fresh and reborn
This is how you make me feel
Midday, dusk and dawn.

Luke Graves

SILENCE . . .

I was awakened by silence
a screaming, agonising flood of silence.
       Informing me of nothing.
       Highlighting oblivion.
       Allowing me no rest from my mind.
Cruelly, this silence surrounds me, engulfs me, laughs at me,
it no longer holds a calming or peaceful quality.

I am unable to stop this silence persecuting and haunting me.

Tonight I lay awake in silence
for fear of it waking me.
       Shattering fanciful dreams.
       Destroying intangible hopes.
       Allowing me no rest from my mind.
Even a brief escape cannot compensate the return to harsh reality
it is less painful to not have dreamt at all.

I will try not to give this silence the power to wake me.

Kerensa Porter

HASTINGS COUNTY (1066 COUNTRY)

1066, that was the year,
     When William came with axe and spear.
In Hastings county landed he,
     The place they now call Pevensey.
Then on to Senlac field they mustered,
     Awaiting Harold, tired and flustered.
October was the month at hand,
     The 14th day the battle grand.
They fought all day, those soldiers brave,
     But mostly ended in the grave.
William was the victor clear,
     With Harold slain, Oh dear! Oh dear!

A Bayeux Tapestry was sewn,
     So the battle could be shown.
William built his Battle Abbey,
     Now a little old and shabby.
A castle too on Hastings Hill,
     Its ruins can be seen there still.
William ruled with Norman cunning,
     To keep the Saxons down and running.
Today there is no Hastings county,
     East Sussex council holds the bounty.
Now tourists flock there to be shown,
     '1066 Country' as it now is known.

C H De Meza

SONNET 1

Who would try to contain their love
All I can say is I know not those
The love that flies as freely as a dove
All blind boundaries overthrows
But with a love such as this
How much of this can one take
But with a secret lovers kiss
Can prove that one is not fake
Why not give all love a hand
Show not all ones hate
Do not let like enemies stand
Two lovers on a lovers date
But as they both do live
let them love, and love to give.

Claire Holloway

THE DEIST

Can I still deny, deny him?
Here, breathless on the southern rim
Of his great, tinged with purple canyon.
Or watch the Sleeping Indian die
Beneath a falling Arizona Sky
And still deny, deny him

Now, in a winter's English tea shop,
Quiet as a cat, wishing the log would drop
And stir the fire. Knowing that special way
Her hand moves out to mine as if to say . . .
Can I deny, deny him still?
Should ever I lose her, I know I will.

Terry Smith

BROTHER

The light shines through the frayed ends
Of the tapestry that is his face.
He has been torn, and re-embroidered
With careful strands of matching thread
(Some a little odd, the colours are so complex)
The pattern followed, the theme copied
From his father's book.
The weaving told the story of his life, as words
Had done before.
But weft and warp were drawn too fine
And now his face is shabby.

Tessa Land-Smith

FOR MY DEAREST FRIEND

All animals are precious
But none so much as mine
United in our aims
As one at Hunter Trials

How could you leave me now
When I loved you, oh so much
Thoughts suffocate my mind
And domineer my dreams

Along with age, come
responsibilities
Of the very hardest kind
Decisions made for others
Are specially hard.

Dependence brings a mutual trust
Providing life with such purpose
But when lost, its emptiness
Consumes our very soul

By design we have good memories
To help provide a cure
And photographs to dwell upon
Only make you love him more

Horses exude life in the extreme
Frolicking for the world to see
Shear power, but so gentle
Pure beauty

My true Passion

N G Wharton

GABBY FROM ABERDEEN

In my old gabby
From Aberdeen
I go to the woods
Where I can't be seen
Practical wind
And sensible rain
Is just the thing
To keep me sane.

Dog takes the lead
And I follow him too
There must be something about navy blue
He's always looking for things to chew
And my gabby is wearing well.

Is there a humbug in my pocket?
I always ate those
At Drummadrochet
But when I moved to Aberdeen
The Northern Lights came on the scene.

If I had to choose
Between wellies and boots
Or pulling up roses by the roots
Between dogs and cats
Apples and pears
Knocking on doors
Running up and down stairs
I'd be all worn and shabby
Like my dear old gabby
Gabby from Aberdeen.

Gillian F Ware

73

RECOMPENSE

Now I no longer rush
For long gone youth's flush
But why fret when past eighty
With each day a bounty?

Time for great leisure
To muse and with pleasure
To marvel at flowers, shading trees,
Mighty mountains, new babies.

Time for friends, family
Warm company,
Time to spread love and cheer
And ever give thanks, - I'm here.

I Simmonds

SUMMER EVENING - AUSTRALIA

The hills soft-etched in the moon's pale glow
Appeared like ships at night on a sea of
Ripened grain that rippled and rolled and soughed
As the light wind gently rose and died.

Came from afar the plaintive bleat of restless sheep
And the sharp harsh cry of a hawk.
Whispers in trees round the homestead, old,
Rambling, shadowy, haunting.

Huge, gnarled, ageless ghost-gums loomed
Silent spectres poised in the creek,
And the cool fragrant breeze softly soothed,
Balmy, caressing, slumb'rous.

Alan N Compton

DREAMING

When e'er I sit by this old garden wall;
Just dreaming to the rock dove's sleepy call,
And see the sunlight chase the dancing leaves
Of silver birch; the bumble-bee that weaves
Its fragrant way among the flower-beds,
Where startled roses toss their haughty heads
Against the summer breeze, I am deceived
By memories my life has not achieved.

Soft summer scenes, which on my senses fall,
Must be the gentle agents that recall,
Through sweet confusion of the atmosphere,
The yearnings of someone who once was here.
Elusive feelings tenderly contrive
A lonely sadness; yet, much more alive,
My soul in that exquisite moment lives
Beyond the pleasure that the garden gives.

The trembling aspen leaf but imitates
The rhythm of the soul which oscillates
Response unto the psychic breeze that blows
Across the borders of the mind, and knows
The loneliness of her who now has left
This temporal garden; her life bereft
Of that incarnate company we seek.
O sweet compassion, why does God not speak?

Pat Tisdall

GUY

The captivation is complete,
With eyes beguiling, smile so sweet.
But Oh! The eyes when he is still,
The signals that he sends at will.

I revel in the brighter signs,
Feel sadness when his health declines,
But varied though his moods may be
I love the sign of each to see.

The worst is oh' the painful sign,
I wish so much the pain were mine.
So small - so frail - he fights so hard,
Provoking love and high regard.

Sometimes his eyes reflect a fear,
When doctors, nurses, hover near.
For as of yet he cannot find
They have been cruel, to be kind.

He shows a trust, and knows no fear.
When those he loves are close and near.
And in a fine contented style,
He gives a truly wondrous smile.

But oh' the joy, the utter bliss.
Just hug him tight, give him a kiss.
For in his eyes it's plain to see
The love reflected there for me.

D Kelly

SITTING IN MY ROOM

Sitting in my room
I am blinded as only I can be
No longer can I see
What you are doing to my world
If I would open my eyes
Should I still be so blind?
Or will I notice the devastation of mankind
The murdering of the different
The man who has got no life to repent
The bloodshed,
The tears wept
Is it worth it to make a point
Has speech become so Neanderthal
Are weapons the last resort to peace
Peace no longer exists in life
In the next life will I want to return
To this world of dark misery
Should I return as a carefree creature
Or in the same world I live in now?
I can't predict the future as only a child
But if in my heart I stay
With my age of innocence
When my friends rule will we be as naive as you?
Will we be able to forget the violence of our youth
When the memory of you
Stays with us what will it be?
Please don't think us so ignorant
We are not blind, as you think.

Alex Mather

POCKETS

Fingers
Delve among the crumbs of what remains
For secrets deep and dark and
Never shared.
Their desperate probings pick
At remnants from the past that cling to nails
For dear life . . .

        . . . Who cared
That what could not be borne
Was fresh fingering of
These fragmentary pieces
Of a life torn
apart?
Fingers that are
Disembodied;
Not apart
Of this warm hand
That took his.
'Take my hand . . .'
'With this hand . . .'
Now it has been returned:
A free hand.

So what can be retrieved
From these unfathomable recesses?
Only a pocketful of emptiness
Held in the palm of the hand.

Jane Dobson

GENTLEMEN OF THE DEEP

Deep down in the cold grey sea
A ghostly shape slips silently.
Amidst the fish
those phantoms lurk
in them *Submariners'* work.

Their submarines of steel
are sophisticated.
Their armoury is perfection
with Laser Beams to point direction.

They are the Silent Service,
We don't know where they are.
These bearded sons of Britain keep
Us safe . . . to live and sleep.

They guard our shores
They keep us free.
The gallant men
of the Queen's Navy.
Gratefully we thank them,
and pray, they will
come safely from the deep,
To see the sun,
Their duty done.
So 'till they go back
Their vigil to keep,
We all salute you,
Gentlemen of the Deep.

Kitty Tomlinson

A DIVIDED WORLD

Cocooned in ivory towers
Some view their lot with pride.
While others in cardboard boxes
Are calling from somewhere outside.

Some draped in silks and satin
Others clothed only in rags
Some carry all worldly possessions
In disposable plastic bags.

There are those who are blissfully happy
And others in depths of despair
Some are surrounded by loved ones
While others have no-one to care.

Some long to know the meaning of peace.
While others revel in war.
Some eat until they're satisfied
But too many are crying for more.

Is there hope for our world today
With contrasts such as these?
Or should we stop and start again
And go back to living in trees?

Cynthia Murrels

POPPIES

A smudge of red on the burnt-gold hillside
the poppies jostle with the ripening corn.
Feathery stalks glisten silver in the sunlight
frail but brave in the stony ground.

Fiery as sunset with petals paper-thin
they sway and tremble in the wind.
Black eyes glance skywards, dancing and bobbing
Nature's first sign summer is nearing its end.

Patsy Jupp

THE PLEA

'Don't talk please'
A scribble on the underside of a top bunk
A bunk on a steamer
A second class steamer
Travelling the Nile
A stretch of the Nile
From Shallal to Wadi Halfa

'Don't talk please'
See him lying there
Fat and thin short and tall
Fair and dark blue eyed
            and brown eyed
In pyjamas and a cotton vest
Cursing quietly in English
(Remember he wrote in English)

'Don't talk please'
Perhaps it saved a row
And a bloody fight
And perhaps they were friends
And one was tired -
- For though it does no harm for
            friends to argue
They should never draw blood

Patrick Tuohy

FASCINATION

There's nothing like an open fire
Cosy and warm on a winter's night
The smell of wood smoke in the air
And flames a dancing merry and bright
Crackle and pop the wood logs go
Ever changing like a picture show
Lakes and mountains rivers too
Colours of a vivid hue
They're all there for you to see
Just like a beautiful tapestry
Then as the minutes turn to hours
They change again to tiny flowers
This time though they're not so bright
They're pale and grey and silver white
Soft when touched, then disappear
Into a cloud of dust, I fear
I like to dream and never tire
Of looking at an open fire.

June Baillie

INSTINCTS

Low she's crouching, watching stealthy,
All her senses keen
Ears laid flat, and tail laid low,
Watching in the green.

Now she's poised, and now she jumps
A flurry there has been,
The prey is caught, and now there's nought
And so it's time to preen.

Patricia Halsey

REMEMBRANCE

I sat and watched you in your sleep
and held your hand afraid to move
the time was close when I would weep,
The last things said were words of love.
The final sigh, your breath was gone
I could not move nor wish to leave,
you were my life my dearest John,
why did you leave me now to grieve?
I could not sleep, the pain too strong
why you, not me, I had it planned!
Each day eternal, hours too long
I'd give my life to hold your hand.
Months of torment and time to greet
need for comfort from those who cared,
travel spent in order to meet
your family, the loss we shared.
A treasured friend has made me see
the things in life a different way,
I cannot stay in misery
my wish to join you fades away.

Jo Ann

GRAMPA SAYS

In my day it was work and no play,
There wasn't time to enjoy yourself,
Working hard day after day,
Not exactly keeping a clean bill of health.

The dust and the chemicals hurt you the most,
And the money wasn't that great,
It wasn't a job you wanted to boast,
Just a job that you just couldn't hate.

Claire Apps (14)

SWINGING LANTERNS

As darkness descended the battle weary
Soldiers sheathed their swords, their shadowy
Figures stumbled out of the valley.
The valley had changed that afternoon,
Changed when the two armies clashed
And the first blood stained the grass,
And the first severed limb fell.
And the first warrior crashed lifeless,
Followed by more and more and more.
The darkness deepened filling the valley
Blanketing the sight but not the sound
Or smell of slow painful death.
Brief patches of moonlight lit the
Serfs and camp followers whose cries
And swinging lanterns stopped as
Master, husband or lover came to light.
The moving restless ethereal mist
Thickened as it covered the valley
Like and eiderdown over the slain.
And the night air slowly cooled,
And the cries of anguish subsided,
And the swinging lanterns left the valley.
The morning sun rose over the crest
Flooding the valley with sunlight.
The mist which had lain quiet
Now stirred and moved and lifted
In a blaze of colour; eager to leave
Freeing more earthbound souls
From another valley of death.

Vic Sutton

OUR JEWEL IN THE CROWN

The garden of England, so aptly named,
What joy to live here, it's not the same,
As other counties, Kent must reign,
Supreme, the prettiest come sun or rain.

The hops grow tall, their smell amazing,
The cows and sheep slowly grazing,
In fields of green and yellow corn,
The flowers colour slowly born.

Poppies growing by the roadside,
Trees so tall, hedges to hide,
The spectacular Oast houses
Where people reside.

The winter months so dull and grey,
In Kent we walk the Pilgrims Way,
Over the hills and through the fields,
To see what produce this earth yields.

Fetes and fairs in every village,
The sun, the droughts, soon they pillage
All the greenness of the countryside,
No more shade for us to hide.

The sun shines bright all over Kent,
The summer months, so hot and spent,
Long dusky evenings, full of heat,
Resting quietly on a Rustic seat.

The spring and autumn are months of bliss,
The daffs' and saplings you cannot miss,
The autumn colours, orange, red and brown,
Kent, the county, our jewel in the crown.

Lesley Martin

THE MEDWAY
(A Kent boundary river)

Speed on divider!
>Between your banks, alive with
>>water rat, wild mink and kingfisher;
flush away the spoil of winter;
home of barbel and chubb and eel -
>>>Spring has come!

Sun, spare the shimmering flow!
>Now host to water-fly and weed,
>>but make the pallid skins to glow
of strollers with their loves in tow;
bring out the dragon-fly and midge
>>to chase each other o'er the ridge -
>>>Summer is near!

Mist and mellow fruitfulness
>bestride the yellowing banks, while
>>blackberry and hips and haws
attracting man and bird that pause,
their faltering breath to strengthen -
>>fewer now as shadows lengthen -
>>>Autumn's around!

Penshurst in snow!
>The river's banks deserted now -
>>anglers and canoeists gone -
year end's deepening gloom has won
as waters rise towards the town.
>>Hold back your flood as rain, pours down -
>>>Winter is here!

Harold Withington

86

A WINTER'S TALE

When I woke up this morning,
my world had turned to white.
Icicles hung from the windows
and snow covered all in sight.

A robin sat in the holly bush,
huddling from the cold.
another sat on my doorstep,
he really was quite bold.

We ventured into the garden,
well wrapped from head to toe.
We laboured most of the morning
building a man of snow.

With coal eyes and a carrot nose
a scarf and Grandad's cap.
His mouth a crooked melon wedge.
He looked a jolly chap.

That evening our garden glistened
in the full moonlight.
It really looked like fairyland,
it was such a pretty sight.

For weeks my snowman smiled at me
and twinkled his big coal eyes
If he'd have raised his hat to me
it would have been no surprise.

When I woke up this morning
My world had turned to rain
My snowman friend had disappeared
Never to be seen again

Margaret J Smith

MEN OF SIDLEY

Men who were boys when I was a boy, hid now in Death's dark cloak,
Remembered still in a Sidley Church, carved names in mellowed oak.
Games which we as children played were childish games of war,
Wooden spears and wooden guns were all the arms we bore.

> Langmore, Rogers, Ridgeway, Tidd, remember those who died,
> Izzard, Errey, Fuller, Beal, remember them with pride.

Boys who were men before their time, their manhood forged in fire,
Gave their lives that we might live, to this do men aspire.
Some ventured forth to foreign lands across a hostile sea,
And came back not to those who loved, but became a memory.

> Nevard, Oaten, Barnes and Grant, do not these men forget,
> Williams, Verrall, Scotcher, Croft, their names re-echo yet.

With clear bright eyes and measured tread, they left their native land,
To die in jungle, desert, swamp, or on Dunkirk's bloody sand,
Their heads held high and hearts aglow, they faced the cannon's roar,
As Nelson, Drake, and Marlborough did in far off days of yore.

> Birnie, Baker, Christmas, Bush, their graves are scattered wide,
> Duncan, Deeprose, Hadow, Hodge, full high their glories ride.
> Stoner, Vidler, Ellis, King, proudly their praises pen,
> For Sidley is, as Sidley was, because of Sidley men.

Norman Cook

REASONS TO LOVE SEASONS

In spring I love the flowers,
and green shoots pushing through.
Snowdrops, daffodils and bluebells,
Cobwebs glisten with dew.

In summer I love the hedgerows,
when bumble bees have come.
I listen to all the birds
who are singing in the sun.

In autumn I love the colours
and smell of fresh crisp air
and berries provide the colour,
when all the trees are bare.

In winter I love the weather,
even wind and rain,
the frosty mornings and the snow,
then spring will start again.

D Brampton

IN MEMORIAM

On the empty
Desolate beach
Tiny pools of water
Trapped between the rocks,
Are all that remains
Of the eternal sea;

The tide has receded,
The glare of the sun
Has faded into twilight,
And the busy day
Slowly ebbs away,
As the little streams
Trickle down the sandy shore
Into a vast emptiness;

So life's day closes
And only pools of memory,
In the darkness gleaming,
Remind us of the living ocean
That in the daylight flowed.

Roy V Whitlock

HOUSE OF CARDS

Why do you bother with me?
All I do and say and think and feel seems to smell of pride.
I walk heading towards the dawn, but arrive out of breath in deepest night;
watch dancing flames but shiver, the reflection quicksilvers away.
Why do I bother even to try?

'Hear me just a little more'

Why do you bother with me?
I shred the sails of the ship that would carry me to Treasure Island.
Solveig turns to dance with Anitra, into the Hall of the Mountain King;
I fall on my party balloons, which burst, like gum all over my face.
Why do I bother even to try?

'Trust me just a little more'

Why do you bother with me?
I build with seeming care, but the cards are sneezed to the ground.
What I touch is dust - it falls to my feet - a desert wilderness forms;
you make me wander in the place I have made - dust adds to dust.
Why do I bother to even try?

'Love me just a little more'

You do bother with me, why?
You stand there, without shift or move, yet still laugh and cry.
Lifted out of the sacking, hidden for a while, I glimpse it again;
a pearl of beauty, a secret deep inside, mine from before and to the end.
Lift me again, and let me try.

You love me always
          never more, never less:
                    So I must listen and lean,
                              how can I not love you more.

Bob Newport

MY GARDEN

I'd mown the lawn, and swept the paths
And brushed the patio too.
The flower beds were weeded.
My long long day was through.

When I went to bed that night
So happy with my day.
I dreamed of my beautiful garden
Charming, bright and gay.

Waking up the next morning. I heard
the lashing rain
Driving through the tree tops
Hitting the window pane.

I looked out at the garden all battered
and forlorn
With leaves and twigs on patio, the
pathway and the lawn.

And as I looked and wondered
It didn't seem quite right
That all the work I'd done before
Was washed out in one night.

I wonder why I bother, I wonder
why I try
But if you love your garden
You'll know the reason why.

O Blanch

OUR HOUSE

At the top of the hill it stands alone,
Surrounded by trees, and a wall of stone,
Our cottage for which we have saved for years
Maturing at last, thro' blood sweat and tears
The low stone wall is covered with purple,
Looking almost like a woman's kirtle
Daffodils, lilac, and tulips bloom
The garden's so small, there doesn't seem room
Bredon, is seen with a turn of the eye
Five humps of the Malvern's are spied in the sky
The birds in the trees, have welcomed us here
There's peace here, at last.

F E Diver

THE MORNING AFTER

I went to the bathroom this morning
To wash as I usually do
And there on my virginal, white porcelain
Were your whiskers, stuck like glue.

My impulse at first was to clean them away
And turn both the taps full on
But there's something quite nice about seeing them there
As evidence after you've gone.

There's a hair on my toothbrush - still dripping
My toothpaste lies raped of its life.
My throw-away razor has been thrown away
And you've just gone home - to your wife.

C Franklin

ETERNAL FLAME

Scrumple paper, plunge it deep
In a nest of shavings and bark.
Build a wigwam of twigs to house it
Then apply a magical spark.
Yellow lick, blue-white dash,
Quietly crumple, burn!
Box in the whisper with dry-wood logs,
And your act of creation is done.

A golden-fingered fire-deva
Tears down the smoke-wood screens
Releasing a riot of eager sparks
In a skyward spiralling stream.
Each wildly flaring fire-fish swims -
There's no need to wonder why -
From the furnace of all creation
To the void of the midnight sky.

Upturned faces love to see
The thoughtless fire-fish ride
From birth to ashy destruction -
It's a glorious, endless tide.
No-one seeks to retain a spark
Or question its part in the game,
Yet still we read those crosses of stone
Engraved with briefly worn names.

Kay Green

THOUGHTS OF SPRING

'Spring at last?
How cold it has been,
Never as warm
As in the past.

The sun always shone,
Birds used to sing
Young men smiled
Oh! - am I getting 'On?'

So! I am not young - alas!
Nor a man,
Yet I find my fancy
Turns to love
For the beauty
All around me.

No sombre news
Of rumoured wars,
Can spoil the grace
Of one green tree,
Now spring is here -
-And we are free.

Joyce Humphrey

MY TWIN SISTER

I have a twin sister she's a pain,
All day long she's the same,
And what's worse I get the blame,
She pulls my hair,
And screams in her chair,
And says it's all my fault.
She grabs the salt
And pours it down my dress,
It makes a terrible mess.

Dad says he'll sort her out,
But all he does is shout and shout,
Shouting doesn't do the trick,
It's horrible it makes me sick.
But I wish she wouldn't always win,
Oh please don't ever have a twin.

Jessica Padgham (10)

NATHAN

Our little boy small and fair
brings sunshine into our lives.
A smile a tear he'll never fear
while we are so near.
We hear when he calls,
we'll help when he falls,
we'll wipe away the tears.
As the years come and go
he'll learn how to show the
love that's grown within him.
Our little boy is like a new toy
because of the joy he brings,
he laughs, he sings, these are
just some of the things which
fill our hearts with love.
Sometimes he's bad which makes
us sad, as when he's good we
are glad.
But for our love we'd never
have had the most precious
gift of all, our little boy so
small, Nathan.

Diane Darby

THE GARDEN

As I step into the garden
The dew still on the ground
I stop and stare with wonder
at the beauty all around
Yes nature is truly wonderful
God's handiwork I see
then can we ever doubt that He
cares for you and me
The flowers nod their heads
As I pass them by
and a blackbird flies over
way up in the sky
the sun comes peeping through the trees
and the roses are swaying in the breeze
the colours are a lovely sight
red yellow pink and white
there will be showers
refreshing they fall
and the garden will flourish
enjoying it all
then when the evening shadows fall
a quiet peace steels over all
the flowers have closed their petals
up tight, as if to say goodnight to all
'tis time for all to seek their rest
then start again revived refreshed.

E Balkham

YOU

Rainbows splash down from the sky
Diamonds of dew glint and twinkle
The wind whispers as it fingers the treetops.
All this when you smile.

The rich earth after rain.
The soft breast of a bird.
Dawn drifting across a silken sea.
All this in your touch.

Comfort of a mother's breast
Strength of a father's arms
Trust in a child's eyes.
All this in your love.

Ann Rushbrooke

WE'VE ONLY JUST BEGUN

Snoring in my earhole,
You rest your tired head
On my comfy shoulder
As you ease me out of bed.

Taking all the blankets,
You're snuggled underneath,
Keeping me awake
By the grinding of your teeth.

Your wind is blowing freely
As it gasses out my room,
You kept me talking all night long
So morning came too soon.

And we've only just begun!

Sarah Maycock

WANDERING EMOTIONS

I'm thinking of you now,
Alone with no one there,
And although I can't be with you,
You know that I care.

My heart and my thoughts
Are not within me,
But instead by your side,
Comforting and holding you.

Inside I am scared
As you must be too,
But it doesn't seem real -
More like a dream.

I pinch myself
And the reality hits me.
You are there, I am here -
Both physically alone.

Our thoughts are wandering -
They meet for a while.
And suddenly, on both our faces
Appears a smile.

Rebecca Goater

THE INTERCITY

Heavy metal Intercity skating down the railway line,
Growling from its engine belly, 'Really must get there on time,'
Shouting through the passing stations, 'Look out there I'm coming through,'
Blowing hats and skirts and hairdo's, turning all the air to blue.

Hastening northwards, swaying slightly, rocking passengers to sleep,
Flashing over level crossings, startling horses, scattering sheep.
Heavy tube of painted metal boring through the limestone hills.
Curling round the swinging landscape, (Jenny's green about the gills).

Passengers encapsulated, flying on through time and space,
Blurring through the dripping country seeing nothing of the place,
Sitting there with thoughts suspended, blind and dull or comatose,
Or chattering idly, saying nothing, unintelligent, verbose.

Speed now slackens, swaying gently, houses take on form and shape,
People stand up, staggering slightly, looking round for coat and cape,
Rub their eyes with mild surprise and recognise their railway station,
And heave a sigh, though life's gone by, at least they've reached their
destination.

Jean Mabey

YESTERDAY

As I wait for the click of the door,
I lie in bed, chasing sleep.
I hear the monster under my bed,
I'm sure I can.
I see its shadow on the wall
Getting ready to pounce.
I scream in terror,
Then in one motion the light is on,
And I am safely enclosed in warm arms.
But that was yesterday.
Today, there's no monster,
No warm arms to comfort me,
Nobody to mop up my tears.
I think of all the times Dad comforted me,
And I wish I hadn't started the argument.
I creep downstairs, open the door,
And rush to the shape watching football.
'I'm sorry Dad, I love you.'
'It's okay now,' he says,
And once more the comforting arms surround me.

Debbie Chadwick (14)

PLACES FAR

All in quiet, tranquil seas,
A raging storm did break,
Anticipating fate at hand,
The very sea did quake.

The sky ruptured, black above,
The ocean rippled round,
And accompanied by silver bolt,
Roared the thunder's sound.

The tiny craft tumbled,
The watery turmoil grew,
And to whip the rain that fell,
A harsh gale blew.

Full fury saw that darkened night
As brine in torrents fell,
A silver eye with horror filled,
A sudden, natural hell.

And off to places far,
The little craft was bore,
As dawn looked down upon that sea,
The craft it saw no more.

Suzanne P Dewdney

SLOW DOWN

Millions of feet, hurrying, scurrying,
Millions of cars quickly speed by,
Modernised trains going faster and faster,
Planes racing sound up in the sky.

Millions of hands, grasping, possessing,
Millions of voices demandingly shout:
Have they no eyes with which to observe life?
Do they not think, 'What's this all about?'

Slow down your pace and jump from the treadmill,
Take time to look at the beauty around;
Take time to give to those who need friendship,
Take time to discover where true peace is found.

Stop rushing around in your purposeless circles,
Which converge in anxiety, stresses and strife:
Take time to spend with your God, your creator,
And find the true meaning and purpose of life.

Jean M Warren

I AM YOUR DAWN . . .

When you choose to wake and feel
The warmth of the summer's fresh dew
Lying moist around your supple flesh,
Then find me as the dawn;
Embraced of life and strong to hold
Keeping in warmth, expelling the cold
Opening the day with touch and grace
Determined to fill your vacant space.

I am your dawn rising soft with the sun
Peeping over the covers as the clouds roll by;
I am your dawn as you stretch and sigh
And move to moan as the minutes fly.
I am your dawn as I caress your breasts
Tangling fingers in your fire probing,
And pull you close and whisper desires
Whipping up flames that fan your fires

I am your dawn, pull back your curtain
What else in life is so certain?

Sarah Chan

GREAT BRITAIN

This is the land that was green and great
Its people were proud their achievements first rate
Nelson Drake and Wellington to name but a few
The list was endless in the days of daring do!

But its people have changed since the days of Queen Bess
The attitude now seems to be 'couldn't care less'
Their spirit is broken the will to fight gone
They seem to despair and that is all wrong

When the bombs came down they all stood together
They fought side by side no matter what the weather
The men went to war the women worked at home
In those dark days this land stood alone

Now war has been won bombs no longer fall
Stop the muggings and murders goodwill to all
Let's all stand together as we did long ago
Look to the future and a bright tomorrow

England, Scotland, Wales, Northern Ireland too
Unite as one together we will see it through
Management and shopfloor there's no time to sleep
Let's get this land back on its feet

Come on you British let's hear your voice
From John o' Groats to Land's End let us all rejoice
Get off your knees stand up and fight again
And put the 'great' back into Great Britain

L P Buckland

NUTS OF MAHOGANY

Acorns, shiny-coated, brittle-shelled
Are fallen from the autumn tree.
Polished nuts of youthfulness
You lie in sheer mahogany
Amongst the spiky grass green blades
Of wooded afternoon.
And here I watch you fall and bounce
Sensing eagerness of mound,
Anticipating egg and cup
They greyness and the brown.
Nutty blossoms, sweet and small
Lying at your father's feet,
One day you'll grace a marble hall,
Crowned - an empyrean window seat.

Ann Safe

SAIL AWAY

I can see you on the other ship,
I can hear your voice afar.
On a wave you drift away
leaving me to be afraid.

I shout, and out I call your name
and you reach out your hand.
A gesture sure, though we both know,
across the sea you flow, I flow.

Feel the flavour, taste the time,
remember it never ends.
I see you stand, you bear the crown;
Don't leave me sailing, for I may drown.

Louise Gomersall

RAPE OF THE OLD SCHOOL HOUSE

The great grandfather clock ticks silently
As dawn floods into the old school room that
Lies hidden in the heart of the South Downs
Of sacred, sensual valleys - solitude.
Yet vulnerable and old exposed to wind
Which sweeps the crisp blue sky and cracks the sun
With shining swords which crack the windows -

                                              crash!

Destroy, despair, decease and driven out
By monstrous motor mouths that spew forth fumes
And flaming fingers, greedy hands
In need of old, of paintings proud, of life
Ingrained in oil, and wood of furniture
As memory of family's peaceful past
Attacked, made meaningless, yet priceless -

                                              cheap.

An empty home in undulating downs
Amid the disarray a whistling wind
Does haunt, yet deep in the old school home's heart
No longer great grandfather can be heard
But silence of the soul

                                         in ashes lie.

Joceline Powter

BRIGHTON BEACH

I've missed you like hell
While I've been out of the shell
Of your love

I walk the lonely beach
Thinking of the times I was in reach
Of your love

I kick the peppered pebbles
And realise I am writing a fable
Of our love

I watch the stormy waves
Batter against the brick promenade
And know now that I'll have to change the verse
To match the beating wings of the seabirds

The v's in the sky circle around
The ultramarine backdrop of sky
Whilst I hold your hand
Just watching, no sound, just colours

The flashing lights of the pier
Come in sight of the eye
Love you

Back to the original verse
Two sentences then
I love you

We sit on the brow of the disappearing ship
Whilst we kiss as if it's a sip
Of the love we know

The mermaid in you has come out
Except there's a revision to my plight
I don't throw myself off the pier
I just die of your love with a tear

Grant Curry

ON RENAMING THE BLUE BOWL, HANHAM, BRISTOL

Blue Baw, say the yokels
In that old peculiar way we have of swallowing our *'l'*.
Ale has been swallowed on the site since Roman times
So you could say the pub is as old as the Bristol *'l'*
(Which is the old peculiar way the locals have of ending their vowels
with a tail.)
The Blue Bowl inn has many a tale to tell.
After the legionnaires slaked their thirst, the Saxons came
And later the Lord of Barrs Court gave the inn a name:
Give me my pipe and ceremonial blue bowl.
No record of any fiddlers in that pre-electric lore
But fighters there have been galore.
Cromwell's men quaffed at the inn before they beat up the Bristol cavaliers
And so did the Grand Old Duke of Monmouth's peasants.
Then they dropped off Hanham Hills.
Belcher made noises there when pickling his fists
And very likely drowned his sorrows in the old Blue Bowl
When he picked a fight too far with big Tom Cribb.
Dick Boy, leader of the Cock Road Gang, slept there with his boots on
But, after a mug too many, his feet didn't touch the floor.
A hundred years later came the war to end all war
And with it the House of Elliott was established for fifty years and more.
Will all of these ghosts be stirred to wish them ill
Who have overturned the Bowl in a Mill House where there's never been
a mill?

Brian Iles

COMPROMISE

When things do not go your way
And you look to lay the blame
On other people's shoulders -
They usually feel the same.
There are two sides to an argument,
Two different points of view,
You cannot say that you are right
Without discussion too.
You really need to listen,
Hear what others have to say,
They have ideas of what is right
But it may not be your way.
That doesn't mean that they are wrong
Any more than you,
So try a little compromise
And see what it will do.

Jennifer Ritchie

TO HEAVEN'S GATE

I thought I saw you in a dream
The like before I have not seen.
I thought I saw you turn and smile
The vision lasted but a while.

I thought I heard you call my name
I looked for you but looked in vain,
I thought I heard your voice again
Like gentle beating of the rain.

I thought I saw you walking by.
You turned to me said do not cry,
Then you were gone you could not wait
Walking up to heaven's gate.

David Hesmer

THE STRETCHER BEARERS

She tells me
That these are
The stretcher bearers,

Thirsty
After the hunt,
Who'll come running

When my hair
Falls out or I
Lose my false teeth.

My God, you can
See the white
Of my knee

Peering from
The gaping hole
In my leg.

And here they
Come, clattering
Their hooves,

Or oozing from
A crack
In the pavement

Beneath my feet,
Like a wry
Will o' the wisp.

Crying empathically,
Breaking their bones,
Bringing bouquets

And candles
Before damping
Their thumbs.

Chris Gibson

HOME-COMING

I was two when my father was demobbed.
Through the bars of my cot I watched
his home-coming, pausing in the room's threshold
to embrace my mother, devouring her with wet
sucking kisses. I would be too young to remember,

or so it was thought. The occasion more a recollection
of a memory than memory itself; a kind of
lantern-slide in time in which no-one moves, where
there is nothing before, nothing after. Silent.

Yet it pleases me to suppose time before.
My mother's anticipation, the nervous
polishing of furniture, brass and chrome,
the freshly run-up frock, make-up, precious nylons.
Then me, new from a kitchen sink bath,
hair crimped into waves by fingers and spit,
unaware.

In the grate would have been the home fire burning,
a conglomerate of welded coals,
suddenly shifting, lazily, like the dry slip
of stacked meringues, the chimney
accepting gladly its gift of sparks.

And the after. From the adjoining room, murmurings.
The bed, unaccustomed to the weight, lets out a crack
and all at once an afternoon sun slants in
making slabs of drifting Woodbine smoke.

Phillip Murrell

WHAT TROUBLES ARE YOU HAVING?

(Dedicated to my mother who was very ill with
glandular fever, August 3rd 1991)

What troubles are you having?
Have you fallen asleep?
Or felt your heart lose the beat.
The pulse in your hand race through the door,
Have you ever felt worse, could you take any more?
Your temperature's risen it's gone through the roof,
A hundred and four you've got the proof!
You're not feeling good,
You're not feeling fit,
You're empty inside,
Your stomach's a pit.
Have you taken your pills?
They'll give you a chance.
Are you sitting on a train racing to France?
It's your summer vacation,
It's holiday time,
It's time to eat,
Time to drink wine.
You're sitting with your friends round the table,
You're feeling better,
You're feeling more stable.
You've left your house spick-and-span,
Sitting in the sun getting a tan.
No use for bottled fake,
You've lost your worries,
Lost your headache,
Get back to England you're feeling fine,
Left your fever in France,
Had hell of a time.

Melissa Pearson

MEN OF KENT

Listen very closely on the dawn of All Saints' Day,
You may hear the beat of horses hooves along the Pilgrims Way.
The men of Kent are riding to their causes once again,
they have risen from their resting place where forgotten they have lain.

Thomas Beckett without the kiss of peace, has accepted Henry's hand.
He is weary now of Clarendon and isolation in a foreign land.
But Henry's empty promise will cause a deadly rendezvous,
he has a meet with martyrdom before the night is through.

Watt Tyler rides to Bearsted to gather all his men,
they are hiding from the moonlight beside the river Len.
He will lead them all to Maidstone, to set the preacher John Ball free,
then on to Smithfield market, where the boy King will revoke his plea.

At Farleigh Bridge the royalists are calling for the King,
They have no premonition of the carnage it will bring.
For Cromwell's ally Fairfax will drive them from their posts,
and in St Faith's churchyard he will sever all their throats.

The castle walls of Allington echo whispered conversations of the past.
They will forever hold the Wyatt's rebellious secrets fast
The successive generations will see seasons in the Tower,
until Sir Thomas's demand for its surrender, will decimate their power.

So do not start at fleeting shadows on the night of Halloween.
Only wonder at the doomed heroes that pass you by unseen.
The land that gave them sustenance enriched their minds with steel.
These Kentish men were bred for insurrection and revolutionary zeal.

Gale Koller

PUTTING OFF WINTER

Finding that October was
Kindly disposed, the trees
Deferred their winter shut-down,
Allowing leaves to continue
Hanging green about;
But as an indication of
The temporary nature of this concession,
Previewed their plan for redecoration,
By displaying the coming season's palate,
Beeswax through Amber to
Sunset-red and Pheasant's-back
On a few models only
And streaking, but lightly,
Other selected specimens.

Haws, rowan and hips, already committed
To crimson, sulked a little,
As leaves continued to preen and gleam
Green, against a sky
As blue as the delphinium,
In a sunshine, still as warm
As the day
The central heating
Was turned off.

Mary Fortune

MY BEAUTIFUL DAUGHTER CATHERINE

I love to watch her sleeping so peacefully and quiet.
Skin as smooth as satin,
Her button nose twitches as she stirs
A big sigh . . . then back to quiet sleeping.

The wonder of her I cannot describe.
My heart aches when I think of how much I love her
The want to live, be alive for her - to be with her - is so strong
Yet I know I would willingly die for her

Often time will stand still enough to reflect
This little being, so perfectly formed, is my daughter
A wonderful miracle of life - the most precious gift that can be given
Being her mother is a role to honour and cherish.

She gives so much joy, so freely, without a care in the world
Running in the garden, eyes bright and mischievous
I scoop her up into my arms, swinging her round -
As she giggles and clings on tight her eyes are telling you 'It's fun!'

My priorities in life have changed and I've discovered why I'm here.
It's incredible how no-one could ever have described to me
- just how wonderful this would be
Yet so many have experienced these thoughts and feelings too.

I tell her often how much I love her, she may not understand words
Yet I know by her sparkling eyes and cheeky smiles that she loves me too.
Her cuddles mean so much, the word 'mummy' melts my heart
My beautiful daughter . . . Catherine.

Louise Thorogood

REFLECTIONS

We grumble and complain
When all we get is rain
There seems to be no beauty anywhere,
The sun has gone,
The skies are grey,
The days are dark and drear -
Running water - dripping trees
That's all we seem to hear.
We splash our way through swollen stream
And muddy country lane, and ask
Ourselves when will it stop -
This rain, rain, rain!

And yet I think, because of this
We treasure still the more,
Those rare and fleeting sunny days
That bring their golden store
Of clear blue sky, and clean fresh breeze
While blowing wide and free -
Comes sweeping down the hillside
Softly stirring grass and tree.
Of brilliance that's all around
And song of bird on wing,
The warmth of sun, and shadows cast
On every growing thing.

This loveliness could never be
Without the rain we hate to see!

Elsie Bradbury

SPRING

Stepping silent, unseen,
Through cool morning air,
Rainwashed and clean;
Touching the pink buds
To gently uncurl,
Spreading sweet perfume;
Then coaxing the woodflowers
To colour the moss banks
With delicate pastels,
Amid shades of green.

Stirrings sharpen the ear,
Creatures scurry abroad,
Invisible, yet near,
Searching to satisfy
Impatient for food,
The hunger of young ones.
Above in the branches
Murmuring breeze
Rocks tiny fledglings,
Whose chirping rings clear.

Starlings squabble and argue
On garden lawn,
Fly startled from view,
Stillness settles again.
Across a lush meadow
Beyond clustered trees,
A cuckoo is heard
Calling to all,
Announcing distinctly
Spring makes her debut.

Carol Mansfield

MEMORIES

It was a green and pleasant land
Where flowers and fruit all luscious grew,
With sun-drenched skies and moonlight bold,
Gave nights of beauty to behold.

Then one day this paradise
With tragic haste was swiftly changed.
All love and laughter fast replaced
By fear and terror and all things strange.

Harsh voices, slaps and much abuse
Became the lot of everyone,
With utter disbelief we knew
They came from the Land of the Rising Sun.

For four long years we did endure
Hunger, death and always fear,
No longer felt like human beings
No comfort, love and much less cheer.

We were so young and female too,
This fact enjoyed with great mirth,
By captors who found much fun
In pointing out this folly of birth.

Sons of Nippon hear us now,
God forgives and forgets,
But you have had our years of youth
And your finest hour spelled our deaths.

Senlac

CONCRETE JUNGLE

The concrete jungle teems
With never ending streams
Of traffic, people, noise and haste
And oftimes it seems a waste
Of time spent on hurrying
Of time spent on worrying
Never time to wonder why
We live and why we die
To wonder on the meaning of life
To ponder on the problems and strife
Of this tortured troubled earth
All this suffering, what is it worth
If there's no time for loving and giving
No time for understanding and forgiving
No time for us to be happy and free
Then what hope is there for you and me.

Sheila Whitehead

DAWN

The minstrel of the dawn appears
Blowing his trumpet loud and clear
Smiling and dancing along the way
Ushering in a new-born day
He skips across the dewy lawn
Waking the birds to a brand new morn
He kisses the flowers and bids them wake
He calls to the fish in the rivers and lakes
He warms the sun that shines so bright
And sends away the dark of night
Then rests, as he sees the day reborn
That trumpeting minstrel of the dawn

Barbara Scriven

TEMPER

He sits there alone,
Watching and waiting,
For what? You may say,
Well he knows what he wants,
And he usually gets it.
His eyes are like flames,
Which burn uncontrollably.
His voice is a sound,
You'd never want to hear.
When he gets hungry,
He creeps slowly up,
And licks his lips,
In a dangerous way.
You begin to feel frustrated and angry,
As a strange sensation,
Starts to take over.
You fight and fight,
But it just won't work.
You're dangerously angry,
Excitably hateful.
Everything, you do after that,
Is evil . . . and black.
He feels happy and contented now,
His deed for the day is done.
You feel calm, yet sad that you,
Gave in to his ways.
You firmly swear that you will never,
Ever do it again.
But he knows for sure, what he wants,
And he nearly always gets it.

Emma Davis

BABY'S WAY
(for Dean)

Look at you my beautiful son,
Full of life, mischief and fun,
Chocolate on your hands and round your mouth,
Not giving a thought of what it does to your health,
Power Rangers, milk caps and cars,
Lego bricks and marbles placed in jars,
What would I think if there was no mess?
Who else could give me such rewarding stress.

Your brothers and sister love you dear,
Even though their pets you taught to live in fear,
And when they can't find things they know,
You only took them to learn and grow,
We love you dearly you're great to have around,
I've told next door we can't turn down the sound,
You'd think they'd be happy to hear you at play,
Fighting, wrestling and screaming all day.

At night when you're asleep I watch over you,
And smile about the things that you do,
It seems just like yesterday,
That 'dad' was the only word you'd say,
Now no one else can say a word,
Because over you they won't be heard!
Sleep well my precious baby boy,
Dream of your next exciting toy.

My family was made so complete,
With the patter of your tiny feet,
And at the end of every day,
I hope this happy we'll always stay,
And when you're a grown man you'll see,
You're still my beautiful baby boy to me.

A Wood

WHERE ARE THEY NOW?

Where the golden stooks of corn;
Where the jugs of lemonade;
Where the farmyard chickens scratching;
Where the pretty milking maid?

Where the shepherd, crook and collie;
Where the milk churns by the road;
Where the sheep fresh shorn by hand;
Where the cart-horse, full his load?

Where the shires in harness straining;
Where the pigs at muddy play;
Where the geese to market driven;
Where the scythe a' cutting hay?

Where the cooper, barrels rolling;
Where the fearful hunting jump;
Where the windmill, fresh corn grinding;
Where the village trough and pump?

Where the hedges, fields dividing;
Where the seed by hand is thrown;
Where the maypole, ribbons flying;
Where the village children grown?

Jane Smart

CHAOS

Then came the builders one by one
Oh what a lot had to be done!

Ceilings down - much plaster falls,
Paper stripped from many walls.

Lucie hides beneath the bed
Comes out only to be fed!

Holly tries out all the paints . . .
Coat turns white, she nearly faints.

Now Roz she cannot find a thing
Oh where, oh where's my diamond ring?

Dirt and chaos everywhere
Cannot even find a chair.

They've burned them up to make some heat
To warm their sweaty, smelly feet!

Eva Smith

WHERE ARE THEY NOW?

Where are they now, those great engines of bone and flesh
and blood and sinew snorting stream into frosty sun-touched
dawns and pummelling earth with piston legs?

Where are their masters, with clicks of tongue and murmuring
voices and gentle hands persuading responses that can open
ground?

What of the tumbrels and wains that gathered loads and creaked
and rumbled on field and lane with grinding iron-tyred wheels?

And hissing delving plough and harrow clatter and clop of
hooves and dungy smells and sweaty flanks and noisy farts
of heavy horses working?

They are still there in places unique, loved by moist-eyed
ancients and gazed upon with new-found wonder by folk
without memories of dusks when horses and horsemen wearily
homed to eat and rest and wait the following day.

John Guerrier

ODE TO YVONNE WHO HAS A 'MAGNIFICENT BUNION'!

Have you ever stopped to wonder
     How those chaps on TV know
If it will be hot and sunny,
     Or if there'll be rain or snow?

Have you ever stopped to wonder,
     As they tell you from their hearts,
How they know which lines and circles
     Should be on their weather charts?

Have you ever stopped to wonder
     At the miracles of man?
How those complicated gadgets
     Tell the weather as they can?

Have you ever stopped to wonder
     If it does take maps and things,
Or if we really do need brains
     To tell us what tomorrow brings?

Have you ever stopped to wonder
     Why the Frenchman uses onions,
When all good meteorologists know
     Best forecasts always come from bunions!

Doreen Stanbury

WHO AND WHERE ARE YOU

I'm sitting here all alone,
Wondering what I should do,
The feeling of total loneliness,
Overpowered by thoughts of you.

The longing to feel your touch,
The yearning to know you're there,
I don't yet know who you are,
How to look; or even where,

Life can get so lonely at times,
Even though I also have fun,
But I don't want to be alone now,
I'm bored of life for one.

One day I know I'll find you,
Best things come to those who wait,
Who can say where I'll be,
I'll leave that in the hands of fate.

Gillian Sims

CUDDLES IN CANDLELIGHT
(Dedicated to Mac)

Home is where the heart is,
So they often say.
Part of mine is with you,
The room near, so far away.
In heaven, you are above
Watching the world below.
Knowing who is grieving,
How we miss you so.
Reflecting on the past,
Loving memories that linger.
We walked this lane now full of spring,
Threw pebbles in the sea.
Cuddles in candlelight,
Words of love we whispered.
It seems like yesterday,
You will always be remembered.
Forgive me is my plea.

Zoë Fail

ENGLAND'S GARDEN

The Garden of England
It's called. So it is.
Whether man of Kent
Or Kentish man,
It all is his.

As a home is approached
Through its gated hedge,
So is England reached
By garden paths
From south-east's edge.

Trees flowers and fruit
And hops for our beer
Bedeck these paths
To London town
Throughout the year.

From coast to capital
It's green all the way
With scenic views all
Unsurpassed
Every day.

The south and the west,
Although excellent
Will never compare with
The beauty of
Our English Kent.

R Hunter

WHILST THERE IS LIGHT

In times gone by
We do not know why
Some folk were made bold
Others left out in the cold
'Twas hard to believe
The truth from lies

When things seem suspicious
Tho' one may not feel religious
Seek the power from within
That keeps one from sin
And seek the spirit
Which gives you merit

When you become older
You will not flounder
Tho' a partner one may not find
Always keep a cheerful mind
Seeking the spirit within
You'll find life has a meaning

There is a definite future
Following the *laws of nature*
Which is never in a hurry
And minds cease to worry
Rejoice while your light burns
For there is no return.

Josephine Foreman

MY FATHER

As I stretch my vision to feel safer
In the dampened darkness of the woods,
My breath escapes, and carries with it my melancholy
For the same thoughts that enter my head
Each time I pass here.
The trees tremble on the soggy breeze
And comfort me like my father . . .
'Wish, wish not your time away, son,
Wish, wish not your time away.'
And I know how safe I would feel,
Entwined in the roots of my father tree.
With his fallen leaves shielding my boy-skin
From the filth and fear of man and the city.
But we breathe the same breeze
And love the same loves.

Simon Baldwin

REMEMBER

Shocked, he rocked the world. Rocked, his eyes locked with
Hers. They fell, spinning, whirling dervishes as one. Each in
Each other's arms, drinking in each other's charms.

Deeper down, deeper down. Round and round. Colours swimming,
Heads spinning, clouded thoughts.
The truth masking lies, shielding eyes. Time ticking,
Trickling, running out on party guests.

Reality loses the edge on fantasy, forgets its head, lies
Almost dead, life blood ebbing. Calling on forgotten memories,
Filling in the gaps. Lies come easily, the end result teases,
Pleases, then leaves.

Scott Johnson

GOLDEN DREAMS

I remember a year of my childhood
And the golden dreams I used to dream
Whilst wandering along the sea-shore
Or by a mountain stream.
I spent so many lonely hours
Beside a field of corn
Listening to the skylarks
In the haze of a summer morn.

I wandered o'er the dunes
And raced the ebbing tide
·To search the rocks and pools
Where crabs and things might hide.
Into my private world of solitude
Companionship I did not seek nor care
For dreams I dreamt in childhood
Were dreams I could not share.

They were such very special dreams
To me so precious and so dear
That I locked each within my heart
To remind me of that year.
But like the melodies of song birds
Or waves upon a shore
Those golden dreams of childhood
Are lost for evermore.

Gwen Liddy

RAPHAELITE

A loveliness came upon me
As I stepped from the summerhouse door
A loveliness I'd imagined but
Never experienced before.
It was like being bathed in a
Warm, clear light
With a smell of the perfumed air
Like being free to respond to
A glorious sight
Of the sunshine trapped in my hair.
It wasn't a loveliness only around
It was something now felt inside
Something I say I'd imagined
Like the joy of an Easter bride
Yet I knew it was all quite true
As it came on me that day
And as I stepped from the summerhouse door
I felt a desire to pray.
To pray that the loveliness always remain
Whether it be around or inside
That the light and the truth would
Always abound and that sunshine and joy
        would abide.
I prayed that quiet prayer, the sun still
        in my hair
I heard a gentle reply
As the wind touched the leaves
Of the cherry drenched trees,
It whispered 'For ever' and
        'Aye.'

Marilyn Dougan

TIME

Time to a child, should mean laughter and fun
For playing outdoors, with a friend, in the sun

Time to a boy, is a bit of a bore
Especially, when kept in by Mum, for some chore

Time to a young girl, is waiting for *him*,
Prince Charming! Where is he? Handsome and trim

Time to a man, is for getting ahead
Raising his family, keeping them fed

Time for a mother, just moves on so fast
First baby, then toddler, to adult at last!

Time to a grandad, is best time of all,
Playing at trains with his grandson, so small

Time for a grandma, is precious and sweet
Her grandchild asleep, in the crib, at her feet

Time for us all, to do what we can
To make this world brighter and safer for man

Time for this nation, to stand up and say
Thankyou to God, for each lovely new day

Kind words and love, not hatred and greed
In time, some will follow, if we take the lead.

Shirley Lewis

HUSH HUSH

Hush hush not a sound
Great white spirit's creatures all around
Racoon runs to nearby tree
Friendly squirrel looks down at me

Hush hush not a sound
Moccasins tread softly to the ground
Antelope in yonder field
From the strong sunlight my eyes I shield

Hush hush not a sound
In the water beavers are found
Rippling, sparkling winding river
Away from me rattlesnakes slither

Hush hush not a sound
I hear the howl of a distant hound
High above an eagle spreads his wings
In the forest a mocking bird sings

Hush hush not a sound
Startled cotton tail goes to ground
Hungry wolf is looking for food
Now silence, peace, restful solitude

Hush hush not a sound
I must avoid the ant hill mound
Buffalo graze not far away
Thank you great spirit for a wonderful day.

John F A Stevens

UNTITLED

You placed your hands upon my head
As into this world I was gently led
A world where you would always be
Right by my side always there for me
Those loving hands they worked so hard
As I played carefree in the old school yard.
You watched me grow, I watched you age
As life just turned another page.
And then it happened, I fell in love
It was like a gift from God above
My arm through yours we walked up the aisle
Every step I took seemed like a mile
You stood so tall and I could see
That you were very proud of me
As time went by the children came
You always joined in all their games
Even then I thought it would be
That you would always be there for me
But then the days grew grey and cold
It didn't seem fair, you weren't very old
So I placed my hands upon your head
As out of this life you were gently led
A greater being from up above
Took from me the father I loved

S Watson

DEATH ROW

How does it feel to be you tonight
As the time of your death draws near?
What are the thoughts that torment your mind?
Is there only room for fear?
Do you dread the lightening of the sky
As it heralds the day when you will die?

Nobody wants to take your place,
Nor to walk with you at dawn,
For yours is the loneliest road on earth
That can ever be walked upon.
How have you coped with your darkest fears?
For you've been on death row for many years.

They say you've been showing some regret,
But what is it all about?
Do you feel in your heart for the sorrow you've caused?
Or just that you've been found out?
Could we believe, if they set you free
That you'd pose no threat to society?

Has God got through to you at all
In these last few months of hell?
A God you'll be meeting very soon,
And who understands so well
The sad disorder that ruled your mind
When you left your humanity behind.

Will anyone shed a tear for you?
A mother, lover, wife?
Did anyone show you love or care
In your badly blighted life?
Sick, sad misfit in society,
Your motives remain a mystery.

Joan Isbister

WE ARE ONE

My soul and spirit fly to the
limitless oceans of eternity.
Nothing, not a whisper of
that which has gone before
can stop the eagle's flight
to its rendezvous with the dove.

Above in the celestial heavens
the dolphins lift up their voices
and sing a song of welcome.
Guardians are they of all that
has been and that will ever be.
And where the sky meets the sea
there is a doorway to our
passage home.

There, watching upon the rays
of light and fulfilment
are those who have gone before.
Radiant, resplendent,
gently smiling in welcome
we come together upon the
chord of limitless time
and merge into the vibration
of all that is.
We are home.

Vara Humphreys

133

WAVES

High waves crashing, tossing,
Throwing, splashing.
The wild sea throwing
Froth and foam into the air,
Or against the rocks, and at
Night when the air is still and
The sea is calm, you can see
White horses galloping along.

Joe Pook (9)

SLEEPY HEAD

When my daddy says it's time for me to go to bed.
I climb the stairs without a word and lay my sleepy head.
Upon my pillow soft and white and I begin to dream.
Of all those lovely places where no-one else has been.
I dream of castles in the sky of Fairy Kings and Queens.
Of silver stars and chocolate bars and tiny babbling streams.
I dream that all the streams are filled with fizzy lemonade.
And all the pretty flowers that grow there in the shade.
Are made of all those lovely things that children like to eat.
Like sherbert dips and candy bars 'Oh' every kind of sweet.
I sit there in my land of dreams with my teddy by my side.
Very soon a bumble-bee will take us for a ride.
Up to the castle in the sky where lives the Fairy King.
As I climb the golden stairs I can hear the fairies sing.
Oh how I wish that I could stay and watch the fairies in their play.
But alas it's time to make my way back to the land of every-day.
But I'll go back to my land of dreams with its chocolate bars and
                                             lemonade streams.
As soon as daddy nods his head and says that it is time for bed.

A F J Wakeford

UNTITLED

I feel that perhaps your distance
is a mask to hide behind,
not really knowing what to say
you use it to be kind.

Instead of telling me the truth
you cover how you feel,
so I am left uneasy,
unsure of what is real.

Today you spoke in riddles,
another game we play.
I had so much to tell you,
but you were just too far away.

I wanted you to know the truth,
I needed lies to end,
I hope that we could reconcile
and more than friendship mend.

But somehow something's different,
what more is there to say?
I see no future here before us,
so perhaps it's best this way.

I suppose what I am saying,
is I've no more left to cry.
I know that this will hurt you,
but I'm sorry and
goodbye.

Jacki Clevett

NEVER THE SAME

Death is a time to cry and say,
your last goodbyes.
One simple sigh and one person dies,
like a blink from an eye.

The day I lost my Nan, was a day when
I wanted to run away.
There was lots I wanted to tell her,
but now it seems as if she has gone away.
Yet someone I loved has been pulled away,
like a person on a string, ping gone, gone for good.
Snatched all the memories, and the time we,
had together.
Now she is gone, it seems like a broken jigsaw,
that needs desperate help to be put back together.

Life will never be the same.
She will never see me on my wedding day.
My life will eventually be the same,
but this part will never be there again.

It's as though someone's eating,
away at my heart, who could be next,
my aunt?

Giovanna Quinn & Danielle Vine

THE OTHER SIDE OF THE COIN

I work long and hard on the factory floor
But every day the boss wants more.
I measure and cut, and drill, and bend,
Waiting for the day to end.
I'm soaked with sweat and covered in dust.
I hate to go on but I know I must.

There's nowhere to put the stuff that I'm making,
The shop floor is full and the whole place is baking.
But never mind! I mustn't despair,
We've record production, there's joy in the air.
The boss in his office is grinning with glee,
As he sits back in comfort - drinking his tea.

Jim Vidler

THE QUESTION

What did they do to our
        country, daddy?
How did they get so far?
What did you do to stop
        them, daddy?
Did you just moan in the
        bar?
Did you not want social
        justice, daddy?
Opportunity and free-
        dom for all.
Did you not try to oppose
        them, daddy?
Did you walk short or
        walk tall?

You had my heritage in
        your hands, daddy
You knew it would be
        mine some day.
They couldn't have taken
        it from you, daddy
So why did you give it
        away?

Derek Powell

THE FLYING FLEA

My pony is nicknamed the
Flying Flea, because he pings
round like a bumble bee.
For a little pony he is very
fast (12.2), he is always in front
and never last.
Sometimes I don't have any
brakes, and when I stop what
a fuss he makes.
He clears the fences quite
easily, he can jump over 3 foot 3.
I love him because he is the
best.
He is also better than all
the rest.

Karlene Elliott (11)

DAUGHTER

> Every minute ticking by, each hour
of every day.
> You brighten our lives in your own
special way.
> Like a ray of bright sunshine, in
a sky of brilliant blue.
> Or a twinkling star, you shine
through and through.
> You're the answer to our dreams, we
could not ask for more.
> You're our dearest little girl, and
it's you we adore.

L Peirce

138

MISSING (DISAPPEARED)

I am a person who has disappeared
Because of pressures which I feared.
No-one can help me in my plight,
I think this way because of fright.

I feel no-one cares about me, or understands,
My worries, my stress, a helping hand?
Can you wonder people are freaked out?
With current trends - you just walk out.

Unemployment, drugs, broken homes and crime;
This is the way it is, no ladders to climb.
No future, no hope, broken promises it seems,
People no longer have hopeful dreams.

You study for a document and degrees -
Ambitions dashed - jobs are freezed.
Older people are no longer important
Self esteem wiped out - one becomes despondent.

What is the point of it all? Where am I going?
I need help but it's all arrow throwing.
Every avenue you explore - anxieties galore.
I give up, there is no more.

These are the reasons why I have *vanished*,
The world is blank and hope is banished.
Why should I struggle any more?
Into oblivion, gone, through the door.

Ellie Collins

PRIORY ROAD PLAYLINK - HASTINGS

Playlink is a vital link,
For our children to play and think,
It brings them together in social skills,
Getting them ready, for curriculum thrills.

Playlink has a lovely atmosphere,
When I called I was in a different sphere,
Seeing the children enjoying themselves,
Different activities giving them thrills.

Playlink arranges home learning schemes,
To encourage a child to really think,
While they are playing, while they are painting,
The patterns of learning are giving them skills.

Having a sing song with Jan and Trish,
Gives the atmosphere happiness,
Playlink is a vital link,
Why don't you come and see what you think?

Having to fight to keep Playlink alive,
Made it important to help it survive,
And now we are happy to continue as before,
Hoping our Playlink will be forever more.

Mary Jo West

SWEET MUSIC

Sweet music how it comforts me,
In times of stress and unhappiness.
Sweet music fills my heart with peace,
It plays so gentle and so sweet.
It calms and enhances my mind.
I feel as one with the sound of sweet music.

From where it comes, nobody knows,
Who thought of it first, and how did it go.
A slight little hum or whistling note,
The beautiful sound of birds.
The crackling of twigs or burning flame,
The sound of waves upon the shore.
Wind rushing through the leaves on trees,
The pattering of falling raindrops.
A gentle buzz of a bumble bee,
Sweet music how it comforts me.

Angela Penny

DREAMS

I dream of seas where the warm winds blow
'Neath a dome of pale blue sky;
Where sunbeams play on silver spray
As cresting waves race by.

And early morn where the green-blue sea
Is touched with golden light;
The warm decks dry in tropic heat
As day succeeds the night.

And on the swell of fresh'ning seas
Where chasing dolphins leap,
The flying fish like raindrops fall
To shower the ocean deep.

Yet in my dream on a moonlit sea
I search midst the luminous foam
For a distant star to guide me true
Through slumbers safe at home.

John Arber

UNTITLED

The lune describes its nightly arc
Across the dappled, velvet sky
And fragmentary moonbeams tell
How owls on silent glide paths fly.

How oft' beneath Diana's spell
Has Bubo swooped with graceful ease
Proposing with a talon poised
A nyctophobic mouse to seize.

But Venus at this vernal time
Invigilates the firmament
And erstwhile hunters willingly
Before the deity relent.

Celestial punctuation marks
Must supervise the sweet refrains
Delivered by the snowy belles
Unto attentive tawny swains.

Otus and Accipitrinus
In long- and short-eared love divine
Beware the latent twilight threat
Of counterglow and gegenschein.

Yet mighty Nimbus orchestrates
A stellar obfuscation
Creating an aphotic stage
For secret nidulation.

O strigene lovers hasten now
Ere Phoebe to her brother yields
And softly sing while you pursue
Your like intent, to wit: to woo.

Malcolm Pearch

DEATH OF AN ORCHARD

It used to be heaven,
        But now it is hell,
The orchard around us, has gone
                and fell,
Pink blossom of apple, spread all around,
But now there's nothing but soil
              on the ground.
Tractors are ploughing to and fro
The soil is flattened, and ready to sow
What will be planted, we've yet
           to know
Let's hope an orchard is ready to grow.

Trish Adams

DOG DAYS

Hot blue, love you,
August time, red wine,
Gold heat, ripe wheat,
Skin taut, taste salt,
Drip sweat, so wet,
Soft touch, too much,
No breeze, still trees,
Deep water, you falter,
Autumn brings, dying things,
Rose tints, sad hints,
Your guilt, full tilt,
Ice blue, losing you,
Hard frost, high cost,
Shatter dream, silent scream,
All gone, so wrong,
Other years, same tears.

Judy Pavier Wilson

THE WORLD

When I look around the world I see,
Such a dreadful place to be.
Rubbish all around the place,
People with an unhappy face.

On the news I hear,
Something I would fear,
I hear of a little pup,
Being tested for make-up.

In the future there will be,
Nothing left for our kids to see.
No more animals from which to learn,
Isn't it time to show concern.

Melanie Froude (11)

NOW AND ZEN

I wait
For my eyes to be the birds
My arms to be the trees
My ears to be the sound
Of rain

I wait
For all talk to stop
From within and without
For all ideas to dissolve
To leave just what is

I wait
For hate and love to leave
For concepts to fade
For all things to be
As they are

A J Mizen

THE OBSERVER

I see the sights,
I hear the news,
from many points of view,
I lift up high not to deny my body which
now wants to fly.

I take off over to discover,
patchwork fields which make a cover,
to hide the long abandoned mothers.

How many wait not just one or two
instead thousands, no more a few.

The women who once bore a nation
now stand and scream in confrontation,
'How long must we wait till all is corrupt
When all that we love can be placed in a cup?'

Whilst everything turns into cement clad sins,
it's no longer an ideal place to live in.

So open the hearts that once could love,
it's not necessary to then fly above,
to observe all that must be seen,
I know there's a balance in-between.
The serrated thoughts that once caused pain,
will one day be made blunt again.

Sarah Mehrabian

WINTER

Christmas is near,
Snow is here,
Ground is icy,
Presents pricey,
Frozen ponds near and around,
Sheep buried in the ground,
Sun is low in the sky,
Snow is piled very high,
Skidding bicycles,
Hanging icicles,
Hot drinks,
Weather stinks,
Nice warm fire,
Coldness higher,
Keeping as warm as you can,
And perhaps build a snowman,
On a sleigh go, go, go,
Going down a hill of snow,
Gloves and hat keeps you warm,
In winter there could be a snow
Storm.

Donna Page (12)

THE 23RD PSALM

Our Shepherd He goes on before us,
Each sheep He loves and knows,
He leadeth us by the still waters,
Our cup - it overflows.

We know that He always will lead us,
Gently pulling us back when we stray,
Guarding the door of the sheepfold,
Lovingly awaiting the Day.

When all the redeemed shall see Him,
And be lifted to glory on high,
To honour the Father, with angels,
Where the pure water of life runs by.

So - drink of this water freely,
The Father gave us the Son,
The pure water of life springs eternal,
Let all who will, come.

Zoë King

THESE ARE THE THINGS

This feeling I have for you,
Here in my heart,
It's getting stronger every day;
Or so it seems,
And every night you fill my dreams;
These are the things that keep you in my heart,
Keep you near to me.

Your hair, your laughing eyes,
Your smile, they make it all worthwhile;
They see me through,
Although they're all I have of you;
These are the things that keep you in my heart,
Keep you near to me.

But you're up there on the screen,
You are a star,
And I'll never hold you near;
Or make you laugh,
For all I have are photographs;
These are the things that keep you in my heart,
Keep you near to me.

Larry Luckhurst

UNTITLED

In the midst of the starry skies
the planet earth survives.
A wondrous living home to share
by animals and life beyond compare.
Nature is its God and guide
which man of course denies.

Man-gods fight to rule the world
from self built pedestals.
Wealth, power and total greed
Fanatical religious beliefs.
Discrimination, exploitation, condemnation
Battles of pointless retaliation.

Increased technology - intellectual stupidity
Materialistically blind to reality.
A chemical world, suffocating, dying
Nuclear power, continual denying.
Pollution, radiation, death and decay
as the ozone layer depletes away.

All self inflicted as intelligence knows
the *immortal untouchables* finance the blows.
War and weapons - the power-man's show
watch as the path to extinction grows.
Personal conflicts take life by force
then there's the threat of the holocaust.

Imagine earth - a barren land
devoid of life by man's own hand.
Blind to the sun, it's dark and cold
eerily silent - the truth untold.
The planet earth will survive
but would its *life* be revived?

S Wise

THE LAST GOODBYE

In dreadful haste, the parting,
Lest buried sorrows rise.
For I'll never see again
Those laughing tender eyes.

With you went the sparkle,
Bright with morning sun.
And with you went the meaning
To life and love and fun.

N M Bowden

THE POWER OF THE NIGHT

So powerful is the power of the night,
It hides everything from sight.
Grass is no longer green,
Just a colourless kind of textured scene.
The trees look like shadows
Or towering demons from hell.
The night can be so still
Or winds can whistle and howl.
In the winds I can hear voices
Calling out to me,
The souls of shipwrecked sailors
Crying out from the sea.
The night shows things that day can not
The stars that twinkle so bright
The moon which seems so white.
Our fears of dark and of the unknown
So powerful is the power of the night.

Adrian Cothard

CATS

Curled up before the fire I lie
Secure and pampered, warm and dry.
I never have to catch my food -
(Or only if I'm in the mood.)
Those tins from which white Arthur feeds
Will furnish all a moggie needs.

My antecedents, by the Nile,
Moved in with man, and by their guile
They earned his worship, lived like lords
Enjoying all that power affords.
In life held up their heads with pride;
In death were mummied, deified.

We've had our ups, we've had our downs;
In Middle Ages cleared your towns
Of mice and rats and other vermin
No soft life then can I determine.
They even burned us with the witches -
Too old to hunt, we died in ditches.

But now our time's come round again
Once more as household lords we reign.
We live with you - you bow to *us*,
And we demand our food and fuss.
If you should treat us with derision
We'll go and work for television!

Winifred Booth

TO JACQUELINE

My little daughter, Jacqueline,
I love with all my heart,
Or do I really love my mien
And try to wreck the start?

Where oh where do we do from here?
My life has come to an end.
I cannot even shed a tear
And for myself I cannot fend,
Oh woe is me, my friend.

A budding author is within
And all my talent gone.
I left it hanging on a star
Ere that the sun had shone.
What doggerel this is, it's sure,
And how can I save my daughter?
By getting on with life, all pure
And doing things I 'oughter'!

Valerie Zenetti-Maxfield

HOW THE YUPPIES ARE FALLEN

I used to be a yuppie with a mobile telephone,
BMW and Filofax and a home to call my own;
a penthouse in Docklands with the river rushing past,
had a six figure salary, never dreamed it wouldn't last.
As the eighties came to a close what had gone up came down
and even Maggie Thatcher was soon to lose her crown.
My lifestyle came to an end one day, I'd been let go they said.
They repossessed my house, my car, they even took my bed.
So now I live in a cardboard box, of past life there are no traces,
but just in case that things pick up, I've hung on to my red braces.

Pauline Brennan

THE UNINVITED GUEST REAPPEARS

There is a house of horror, a house that's haunted
Spooky, damp, dingy, bleak daunted
Ideal conditions weaving your magical snare
Intricate network spun with fanciful flair.

A palace of prestige, the perfect palace
Artistically decorating chandeliers without any malice
Maids invading your privacy with one swift move
With eight amazing legs a strong character you prove.

The colossal castle, a castle that's cold
Dungeons, towers to explore ancient so old
Hiding places, safe places behind the iron gate
Silently spinning a silvery web enticing unsuspecting bait.

A country cottage, a cottage that's cosy
Enchanting, quaint, carefree, warm and rosy
Seized, suffocation, a matchbox you endure
Thrown on the velvety lawn, lucky to survive I'm sure.

The magnificent manor, the manor for a millionaire
Hate, love or loath you, putting in an appearance anywhere
With the speed of light, silently avoiding superficial lords
Weaving, darting, crawling through a maze of oak boards.

A house that's new, a house that's old
An uninvited guest you won't be told
Your favourite place, a classic, the bath
Horrifying the occupant, sliding the slippery path.

My home, humble home, home sweet home
I've always liked you, letting you roam
Despite hysterical shrieks the deafening tone
So please, leave my girls' room alone!

Hazel Smith

WONDERING

Sitting here I watch you sleep
Like an angel that cannot speak
I wonder what you really think
When I see your eyelids blink
Do you think or do you dream
When you smile it's with a beam
Watching you grow is a joy to see
What in your life will you be
Your skin is like a satin sheet
Tiny hands tiny feet
I often wonder what it was like
When I was small as you alike
One day you will learn to speak
But as for now an angel asleep.

Steven Cannings

THE SPRING GARDEN

I walk the garden in the spring
Observing life in everything
I see shoots breaking through the earth
And wildlife waiting to give birth
The frogs in the pond laying their spawn
And baby rabbits playing on the lawn
The graceful willow weeps in the breeze
As flower buds swell on other trees
How I love the spring in my garden here
Making this my favourite time of year

Joan Boakes

VALENTINE CARD

If I told you I loved you,
What would be the result?
Would you be flattered,
Or take it as an insult.

Would we carry on being friends,
The way it was before?
Or would you hold it against me,
And not talk to me anymore?

If I asked you out,
To go on a date?
If you turned me down,
Could I still be a mate?

Is it worth taking a gamble,
And blowing the lot?
So I will write 'love anonymous',
Original or what?

Jason Foulkes

OBSERVATIONS

Crossed wires,
Empty spaces,
Confused minds,
Deserted places.
Using, abusing,
Lies and ties.
Fighting, dying,
This is our lives.

Alex Hodge

TESTING FAITH

There's meant to be a God
Around us, everywhere
A God of love and goodness
A God who really cares

We're told that He's almighty
He makes the world revolve
Everything is down to him
At least that's what we're told

But where is God in famine
Where is God in strife
Why does he let the bad things happen
In everybody's life

And where is God in the disasters
Which happen now and then
And take the lives of many
Tell me, where is God in them

Stella Froude

AN ANGEL PASSING

Silence fell like a stone
into the pool of laughter.
Heads turned slowly around,
apprehensive of what might come after.

Breath was restored and released
in a gentle zephyr-like sigh,
with a quizzical smile of relief
that an angel was just passing by.

Damson Templeton

COUP DE FOUDRE

There was yellow thunder over the wood
and the trees were singing their symphonies,
when the lightning struck.

It came
on a backdrop of crimson sky,
with a curtain of purple tears;
sweet fanfare of love.

You were there with me,
strange, and eloquent.

Your body was a caress,
your lips were fire,
and your mouth resounded with my passion for you.

Your tongue was a foxglove, seeking mine;
and, whenever our fingers touched,
we turned ourselves into honey.

When I spoke your name, water flowed,
and the sky flowered in lilac clouds above us.

Patricia Marston

CHRISTMAS DAWN

The frozen meadows are covered in a cruel white,
The grass a mass of frosted silver blades.
Mud too cold to cling
Crunches beneath my feet.

The first glow of dawn rises above the copse.
The skeletons of trees await the spring resurrection;
Still silhouettes against the sky,
Not dead but sleeping.

The sun reaches down to give a warming touch,
Transforms the earth to fields of glistening diamonds.
Soon jewels of every hue
Sparkle in the sunlight.

Steam clouds from the gravestones rise heavenward.
Memories fade like the letters once engraved.
Here lies the death of many dreams,
The hope of many more.

Andrew Hinchliffe

THE HIDEAWAY

Today I revisited the diner,
the old place, our hideaway.
Memories poured from the emotion soaked walls,
lapped my feet
and seeped up through the grain of my being.

There came a presence of former friends
who had shared my lot
when a note was made of each our woes,
then repaid, and ne'er forgot.
But youth seems so much older now
and liken to them I cannot.

Tomorrow I shall revisit the diner,
the hall of masquerade,
Peggy's hideaway.
I shall sit alone amongst others
and without judgement or desire
I shall sense the change
that comes from permanence.

Jon Farmer

DEEP INSIDE

Just another day, just another way,
for this painful life, to twist and turn the knife,
for the knot inside, to become firmly tied,
and the world moves on, but all feelings gone,
at the walls I gaze, through translucent haze,
transfixed by pain, almost insane,
pushed to the brink, just sit and think,
it's all that's left, of a life bereft,
torn apart, this bleeding heart,
my strength is drained, where once it reigned,
tiredness fills my head, be better off dead,
now I'm alone, in this empty space called home,
stillness fills the night, love's lost its bitter fight,
my return to life no longer yearns,
deep inside its flame no longer burns.

J Stanbury

CONUNDRUM

When we, as one, together lie,
I fake the carnal deed.
Demeanour void of honesty,
My purpose; to mislead.

Whilst in your arms this game I play
Of feigning and deceit.
Contort impressions to convey,
The trickery complete.

I allege and I imply.
I make believe with you.
Despite you are not mine, still I
Pretend you love me too.

G Lewin

THE CAR BREAKER'S YARD

Silent it stood in the cold winter rain
And its cooling heart would not beat again.
Fading paint on a once cherished shell
For this one last drive to the gates of hell.

Its owner gone. Sadly walked away.
Stiffly, slowly in the fading day.
Unhearing the din of disembowelment;
The crunch and shriek of last lament.

But crowding echoes of far away:
'Full synchro? 76 in top? I say.
'When she's full run in we're going away.
Down to Bournemouth for the day.'

'See how she flies up Primrose Hill?
The way she went along the straight! What a thrill!
How bright her lights on moonlit nights,
And how secure the feel through her steering wheel.'

'Now go easy on her son. She needs a rest.
Remember you've only just passed your test.
Get Kay back to her mum and dad
And don't do as I did when a lad.'

How we swooped and climbed that night. Did we have fun!
But a whispered voice said 'Your race is run'.
Now silent I wait in the cold winter rain
And my cooling heart will not beat again.

L Upton

159

NEAR CANTERBURY

An offshore hot summer's breeze
flicks ripened corn and raiding sparrows
into past pathways only to appease
hidden, sleeping Bronze Age barrows
where the much overgrown ancient footpath narrows.

Further inland a smock-mill
welcomes stirring of the windy waves
because its greyish sails are standing still
as it cunningly surveys
a cemetery of buried Anglo-Saxon graves.

Nearby the old witches' stool
rusts and still innocently wages
over the clear stream, now a stagnant pool;
empty since the Middle Ages
no longer dipped with inflammatory rages.

On the nearest motorway
clouds of crippled air meet present man
and buried toxin under yellow clay.
From *vici* to *oppidan*
the landscape had to live with him since time began.

Etelka Marcel

PLEA FOR PEACE AGAIN

So many years have passed us by,
But still our prayers we send,
When bombs and murders cause the tears
At human life's sad end.
The terror and the suffering
Still play a major role,
Come church, come politicians, now
Please help us reach our goal.

May we not put our hate aside,
And live in peace as friends.
Let tolerance please be the guide
On which our lives depend.
This anger tore us all apart
Throughout preceding years.
Let's put aside our differences,
And cast away our fears.

Amanda Howse

MY BROTHER PAUL

Me mam's gone out and left me to sit here with our Paul
He's me brother and he's just two, I'm not keen on him at all

Me mam's gone down the bingo and left me all alone
She said if it rings don't answer it I think she means the phone.

I will have to change his wotsit, that towel wrapped round his bum
And you can bet your life I stick the pins right through me blessed thumb.

Me dad's gone down the boozer to meet me uncle Sid
He won't be home till closing time he don't care about the kid.

Me ma will be back at eleven I will hear the key turn in the lock
If the kid ain't fast asleep in bed I won't half get a clock.

If me dad comes back and he's drunk and me ma has won a packet
I think that I will go to bed 'cause they will only cause a racket.

Me dad will want the money and me ma will hang on tight
and you can bet your bottom dollar it will turn into a fight.

So me brother Paul and me will be sleeping tight tonight
Unless the little bugger cries 'cause I have turned out the landing light.

So let's hope me dad is sober and me ma ain't got no money
'Cause with any luck the pair of them will be as sweet as honey.

Lynn Barry

SPRING

Sweet spring, you darling babe,
You precious gift from God above,
Radiant, pure, refreshing as the
Dew on leafy evergreens,
Your contented smile, while feathered
Angels sing their songs of love,
Mid bursting buds, and spiders' webs
Of silver sheen.

Oh spring, why is it so, you make the
World so full of love and passion,
Animals, birds, and humankind,
Go into loving ecstasy;
The stately tree, a nature's child,
A child of your own fashion,
Bursts forth to life, a vivid green.
To full capacity.

Mother spring, you giver of life,
Your loving arms caress the world,
North, south, east and west unfolds
Your beauty spreading fast,
The morning sun, o'er a wooded hill,
With fields dew pearled,
Tells all God's children, now awake,
The cold grey winter's passed.

F N Watkins

LIFE

The wind's breath touched me.
I was kissed.

The air seeped into my skin.
I was polluted.

The sun shone upon me.
I was slowly killed.

The soil covered me.
I was forgotten.

G A Ling

A POEM WITHOUT A NAME

Through long grass and fields
Full of poppies
And summer days long gone by.
Daydreams that continue forever
Down valleys that lead to the sky . . .

And flowers with petals like teardrops,
That languish but never cry,
Near the place where we lie till the sunset
Spinning words
Like fine cobwebs in the sky . . .

And at times we have all been immortal
And thought we could never die;
And we'd laughed with a blessed complacence
Till we'd cried from the fear of goodbye
And I whisper it now from the sky . . .

J A Maskell

MORNING AWAKES

A gust of breeze stirs the trees
And sunlight shines in narrow lines,
Amidst the clouds, cold and grey,
Sending forth an orange ray.

Melting mist and morning frost,
Translucent scenes to all are tossed -
A message meant for everyone,
Dull night is drowned by morning sun.

Annette F Brannon

OVER THE BRIDGE TO SKYE

Dear all. Bumping along.
May grab a tow.

Strange being on me own
but as you know

you guys would cost a bomb
crossing to Skye.

Much less for me on wheels
so you chose why

am rolling on me own.
Could drive you mad

or up the wall
not having me around

but don't go far
'cos if I stall I'll phone

for yous to come and fetch
yours truly 'car'.

Rosemary Keith

SILVER CANDLES

You showed me silver candles
That glistened in the moon
You promised more of everything
If I would play your tune
Yet I was much more versatile
And made music of my own
But my notes came to nothing
As you have now been shown.

My hands would flutter the keyboard
Fingers could work so soft
And music would take over
When everything else was lost
To play, to play, to play, to play
Sounds soaring into space
Chords laced with floating magic
Would mesmerise your face.

Now I'm left to amuse myself
I refuse to listen alone
Locked in a crescendo of feeling
The melodies enter the room
But the sudden staccato of loneliness
That creeps in at the end of the day
Reminds me of those candles
Before they were burnt away.

Eileen Sanders

THE OWL

Sentinel of secrets,
Sitting there so bold,
With brown speckled breast
And beak of gold.
What do you see
With your sharp beady eyes,
As darkness envelops
The earth and skies.

Are you waiting
For some unsuspecting prey
To store away
For your meal next day?
Are you thinking of us
Sleeping creatures below
Or solving your problems,
We do not know.

Your shrill piercing hoot
Is all that we hear
Breaking the silence,
So loud and clear.
You stand as a symbol
Of all that is wise,
What then of your thoughts,
We can only surmise?

O creature of night,
O sleeper by day
Will your secrets
And dreams always stay
Locked in your heart
Till the break of day?

Jean Humphris

THE WHIRLPOOL IN MY LIFE

I was a child innocent and happy playing in the sea,
Content with the world and had done no wrong,
Then anorexia came along and pulled me down,
Like a whirlpool - it was fast and vicious.

I tried to escape - but further down I went,
I stood alone - so no-one saw
Down I went - further, further with no escape.

Drowning in my despair the frustration grew,
My body had no chance to escape,
But I continued to fight - I wouldn't give in,

The whirlpool continued - round and round,
My feelings so strong and hard to beat.

Helpless, helpless is how I felt,
The whirlpool in my life, was oh so harsh,
Evil, hatred it seemed to me,
But I knew that only I could set myself free.

I was tangled up, in so deep,
My energy was going, with little fight left,
Down, down my body went - until *gone* out of sight.

But then I saw a glimpse of light,
Was given some energy to help me fight,
And as I fought I slowly rose.

I was given strength, and I found the courage,
The whirlpool stopped and let me walk free,
I stood up tall and walked away from that evil, hated sea.

Tracey Wheeler

A STORM OVER KENT

They said there would be a storm today
And across the Kent coast it looked a bit grey
The sky got darker as the day went on
It is not often the weather man is wrong

A roll of thunder is heard in the distance
Clouds no longer have any resistance
Lightning flashes over the Kent coast
Such a beautiful sight I have to boast

The rain hits the ground at a frightening pace
You would think the droplets were in a race
They come to rest with a terrible thud
Turning summer dust into thick dark mud

Men and their boats are moored in the bay
Animals and birds hide themselves away
Waiting patiently for the storm to pass
And the sun to come out and warm the grass

The skies over Kent are now turning blue
Clouds are gone and everything looks new
Birds start to fly all around the trees
Soft winds blow gently causing a breeze

I sit at my window and cherish the sight
Of my part of the land so clean and bright
But it does not belong to me it is only lent
This garden of England my county of Kent

Celia Law

PARENT TO CHILD

Something I thought I would never say,
but now I'm a parent it's as plain as day,
things were different when I was a child,
the things we got up to were much more mild,

But let's try not to make such a fuss,
come on mums and dads it's up to us,
let's give our kids a sense of fun,
from father to daughter and mother to son,

So what if they can't walk alone down the street,
there's plenty of places for their friends to meet,
let's not give them adult worries and strife,
but befriend our children and give them a life,

Children are not animals that live in herds,
they are little human beings more precious than words,
I have childhood memories that will never go away,
Potato printing and people made of clay,
camps made from blankets and grannies best chairs,
and oh those marble runs from the top of the stairs,
dressing up as pirates and jumping on the bed,
mummy's face and the things that daddy said!

You just have to do some remembering,
to how it used to be,
things aren't so very different now,
than it was with you and me.

T James

FACE AT THE WINDOW

I sense him at the window, more a presence that is felt,
And I can't help but wonder what to him his life has dealt.
To live his life in shadows, sheltered by a curtain's lace,
Hiding from society, just a face like any face.
What could be so bad to make a hermit from this guy?
Just sitting at his window watching life just pass on by.
Does he have a family? And did they leave him there?
Do they know he's on his own, or don't they even care?
Has he been a father - did he give the gift of life?
Has anybody cared for him? A friend? A son? A wife?
And left him on his own like that, just sent him on his way.
Or is he just another victim that typifies today?
What goes on behind those eyes? What does he think about?
Disdain at what the world's become with streets now full of louts.
Did he risk his life at war? Did we mean that much to him?
That he would stake his very life to make the war our win.
Did patriotic spirit help to carry him back then?
The day he had to hold a gun and aim at other men.
Did he do this all for us so we could have a home?
Sacrificing morals to keep Britain as our own.
Then, when it was over, did we then reward with fear?
And did we scoff him on the street whenever he came near?
Is that why he's on his own - we've made his home a jail?
And did we sentence him to life, with no reprieve of bail?
And I can't help but wonder every time his face I see,
Does he do the same as I and wonder about me?
Does he hope there'll come a time, I'll stop and say hello?
Or is that what he's dreading, would he tell me then to go?
Or will I wait till it's too late then stumble on a day
His window's finally empty; to find out he's passed away.

Debbie Neal

170

SUNSET

Beautiful sunset
Please don't die
Shades of blue striking pink
And orange
Wait for me.

A single bird flies
Into the depth of your fire
Silhouetted dark and defined
Against the furnace glow
Of the day he's chasing.
He's trying to preserve it
To keep you alive
But the life's blood is sapping
As the night keeps up its torment
And you beautiful sunset are giving way
Unable to offer resistance
You can't fight the way things are
You have to die
To let tomorrow live
This time like yesterday
I'll stay for tomorrow
But one day I will come with you
And that day we'll fight the night together
And we'll lose like always
The way things are

Your colour fades
Your light is gone
Night is come
You died.

Jeremy Roberts

ORANGE AND GREEN

By God's own hand
We're on this land
To till and sow
And reap the crops.
To work and care
And nurse our young.
Nourish each other
And protect our loved ones.
We're all different colours.
Some black, some white,
Some orange, some green.
But underneath,
We're all the same.
God's children,
You and me.
He sent us here
To do His will.
By His own hand
We're on this land.

Alyson Jones

DEAR FRANCES

Again no letter; just a bill, unread:
Another day, a desert, lies ahead:
I've tried to work, but concentration's flown.
Where are you?
If you can't write, then why not use the phone?

I'm not possessive, but I'd like to know
Just who you're with, and everywhere you go;
And what you say, and what you think, and wear.
Where are you?
Tell me all, then I'll say I don't care.

Michael Irish

HAUNTING REALITY

Midnight strikes: Again I see her
as she glides across the room,
weighing each graceful movement,
humming the same sullen tune.

Oblivious to my being there,
bemazed in a world of her own,
eyes vacant, all hope lost,
blank expression - the colour of stone.

By candlelight I watch her
retracing steps of yesterday,
reality frozen in the air,
she stares, but has nothing to say.

Who was she when breath was fresh?
A dreamer, a thinker, a fool?
Was she brave or cowed by life,
compassionate or heartlessly cruel?

Craving to know, why does she come?
What memories could this place hold?
Perhaps of life, maybe of love,
Or is this where her body grew cold?

Gazing intently into the mirror,
enchanted, I follow to see;
pale face that reflects - I know so well:
The only ghost in the room is me.

Alida Moon

THE WORLD

God made the world for you and me
He made the earth the sky and sea
The sun snow and refreshing rain
Animals that roam the plain.

He gave us day He gave us night
He gave us all the gift of sight
The blessing of a restful sleep
And all our sowing we may reap

The birds so graceful as they fly
Clouds float by in the sky
Starlit nights and sunny days
The waves that wash around our bays.

The trees in spring their leaves unfold
When autumn comes they turn to gold
Summer flowers fruits and berries
Apples plums and sweet red cherries.

We came upon this earth for this
To live a life of peace and bliss
We must preserve and guard it all
If we fail the world will fall.

B Z Brown

THE SMUGGLER'S RUN

Bring the ponies down the beach lads
and hang your nets up to dry
for tonight we haul a richer catch.
Be careful with the cargo boys
as we wade through the shallows,
for the profit in them barrels
will fill your young 'uns guts this winter
and keep the bailiffs from the door.

By cart and old owling tracks we go
before the turning of the dawn.
A keg of brandy for the local rake;
around the back now, quickly be,
for on the morrow he may sit before us all
upon the magistrate's bench;
and pray the devils on the marshes
keep the customs men from our backs.

Michael Wilson

NO KEYS

From where they come,
They'd rather not say,
All have troubles,
That won't go away.
Life in a box,
Holds no meaning,
The chill bites back,
Disrupts the dreaming.
The fumes lie heavy,
Out by the road,
They can't sign on,
With no fixed abode.
Without four walls,
And not much more,
They have no hope,
So don't ignore.
They need your help,
The people from nowhere,
Help release them,
From the nightmare.

S Beach

LUCK

From the moment of conception
Lady Luck is there to start
Waiting in the wings
In life to play her part
To most she gives out luck
A mixture of good and bad
To others a surfeit of either is had
Beauty, brains, and talent
To some she gives for free
Whilst hard work and dedication
Are rewarded with perhaps, or maybe
Health, wealth, prestige and fame
Are pearls given out in her little game
So when the roulette of life she has spun
No matter where the dice may fall
In humans, hope springs eternal
Without it, there's no life at all

Ruby Darling

A TRAMP'S TALE

In my tattered overcoat, old hat upon my head
Along the city streets I walk, for miles and miles I tread
A parcel tucked beneath my arm, which carries all I own
My nights I spend in London, 'neath the arches, all alone
The bottle in my pocket acts as my only friend
My only shoes have holes in, which I can't afford to mend
At the bottom of the station steps, stand I, with outstretched hand
Hoping for some money from the people dressed so grand
Once more beneath the arches, my weary legs I rest
And fumble in my pocket, which holds what I like best
My life is free and easy, I lead it how I choose
Some meths and one brown parcel, is all I have to lose.

Alie Fish

176

SPRING

Spring is here again,
Blossoms bloom the same,
Flower petals open wide,
Along the rich countryside.

Daffodils and tulips peep,
From their deep winter sleep,
April comes in little showers,
Then the sunshine and the flowers.

Lovers walk in the glade,
Among the trees in the shade,
A bird sings on a bough of a tree,
All around it is beauty you see.

The bees buzz from flower to flower,
This they do for many an hour.
The birds build their nests and sing,
This is surely a sign of spring.

Trickling streams and rivers flow,
Gusty the spring winds blow,
Gone is the winter and cold,
Spring is here strong and bold.

Playful lambs skip and run,
Full of life and full of fun.
Young and old welcome spring,
The woods with bluebells ring.

Now my story has an end,
So I a goodbye will send,
As summer makes her start
And cupid has thrown his dart.

Elizabeth De Meza

WINTER

Winter wears a harsh and cruel face
When frost paints windows, icicles fringe eaves
And winds like knives slash through the trees' black lace,
Whipping away the last few withered leaves,
Driving the stinging sleet with fierce delight
While iron-grey clouds crouch threatening overhead
And water, once alive and mirror-bright,
Beneath its icy sheet lies cold and dead.

But when grim winter's rare warm smile breaks through
The earth is held in a more kindly hand;
Snow-quilted meadows glisten silver-blue
And radiant skies transform a sun-starved land
Into a magic world of sparkling light
Where children taste the thrill of slide and sledge,
And holly, decked in scarlet, green and white,
Hangs Christmas decorations in the hedge.
Cats leave the fire to bask on sunny sills,
Squirrels awake to seek their hidden store,
All memory of yesterday's bleak chills
Shut out, till two-faced winter frowns once more.

Jeanne Snelling

UNTITLED

I've been fortunate most of my life
With a comfortable home and contented wife
It's not many can say that in this day and age
When argument and divorce are all the rage.

We do have differences I must agree
And I often wonder what she saw in me
Was it the uniform, that fitted so trim
Or the dark curly hair and body so slim?

Or was it my smile that did captivate?
And make her realise, I was the ideal mate
I've done my best in good times and bad
With the same brand of humour I've always had.

She's heard the same jokes so many times
And can still raise a laugh at my verses and rhymes
What more can I ask, so late in my life
Than to be blessed with such a faithful wife.

V G Relfe

AUTUMN SONG

See the leaves as they fall down
Some golden yellow some golden brown
They gently fall down upon the ground
It's here it's now it's autumn all around.

Now lays a golden carpet where there was green
The wind softly rustling the falling leaves
There'll be lots of chestnuts laying side by side
And the cool crisp evenings will have arrived.

The colours of summer have come and gone
Now the colours of autumn will sing their song
The season is changing to russets and browns
An autumn glow lays all around.

The many birds that gather on the trees
Know that now's the time that they must leave
To travel south and find warmer skies
They are singing their songs that say goodbye.

In the woods the squirrels are down on the ground
And they must search all around
Their foodstore they must build up high
Before the winter comes a'nigh.

Christine Spurrell

WAITING

The bark of the fox is in our land
and the hills are white from where I stand.
The crisp crunch of snow is on the ground
and the husky bark is the only sound.

The morning light is a fearful white.
Quiet snow has kept the birds from flight.
The sudden softness of its fall
has frozen silence in us all.

Even the fox who pads back home
as heavied trees bend down and groan,
is wearied by the snow so deep
as I stand and silent vigil keep.

With people sleeping all around,
no rousing voice can yet be found,
no voice to take away the fear,
no-one to fight for things held dear.

Where did liberty and freedom go,
why wait and wait beneath the snow.
How deep below down in the earth
do seeds of hope await rebirth.

The fox and I, we feel it now,
as does the tree with snow bent bough.
Let the wind arise, let them stand.
Let the bark of the fox arouse the land.

Ken Simmons

DEATH OF A FRIEND

Friend, you're free now,
Free as the fresh wind
Touching my cheek,
Forever and ever on the moving breeze,
Flying in the feverless free air.

The bluebells are out now
Friend, blue and fragrant, deep
And bluing the corn edges,
Green, under the ferny sky,
Eternally young, content, serene.

Friend, see them now,
Through my eyes; feel them,
Remember and remember,
No pain to heed or hinder,
Nor sorrow, to jade.

And when they fade,
Friend, like you, they renew
In splendour, another time,
Another place, the same and
The same blue love, and true.

Friend, hear the trees now,
Through my years, listen,
Echoes of joy, cooing and wooing,
In shadowful evenings,
For generations to treasure - singing,
I'm listening, I'm listening.

D V Powter

WHY

Why did our Lord refuse to be
saved
As they paved his way to the cross
that day

His only crime was giving away
Love from his heart for us to
Be saved.

He brought the light in every way
To thousands of people who knelt
To pray.

Why was he the one betrayed
As they nailed him on the cross
That day.

Greed and corruption these are
The things when man sat in
Judgement of one who's a King.

J Torr

TO BECOME

All is still,
Quiet, tranquil.
A flutter of breeze,
A movement of trees.
Restful, relaxed,
A small world perplexed,
Change, modify,
See through the sky.
Elements falter,
Time to alter.

Sandra Godley

A SUSSEX LANE

I know a little lane, which winds and wanders
                                    'neath the hills.
An ancient lane, a peaceful lane, where people
                                    rarely go.
On grassy verges in the spring, softly the sunlight
                                    spills.
And hawthorn hedges whitely gleam, with blossoms
                                    all ablow.

The golden catkin tassels fling their pollen on
                                    the air
And the pale primrose blooms there, with its
                                    wild woodland scent.
Sweet are the wild violets, and pure as a
                                    nun's prayer,
And oft may I their fragrance smell, e'er
                                    all my days are spent.

The purple orchids gleam like flames, the
                                    cherries meet o'erhead,
And delicate the beauty of the lovely Queen
                                    Anne's Lace,
The bluebells ring their faery bells, a man's
                                    soul must be dead,
If he should fail to thank his God for all this
                                    joy and grace.

Green are the hills, and lovely, scented with
                                    thyme and sweet,
But lovely, too, the little lanes, which wander
                                    at their feet.
In springtime, when rose campions bloom, on
                                    nutty autumn days,
In verdant summer's leafyness, their beauty
                                    I will praise.

Molly Combridge

BELLA DOG
FLUFFY BLANKET
KITCHEN
ANGIE'S HOUSE

Dearest Bella
   I hope you know
Just how much I love you so
I think of you when I am not there
Your soft brown eyes and silky hair
Sorry when I am feeling blue
I sometimes scream and shout at you
Please believe the fault's with me
Things sometimes get so bad you see
Hope you can forgive my mood
I really don't want you to brood
Have a peaceful happy life
Free from having too much strife
Soon the weather will be hot
We both will play outside a lot
Enjoy the sunshine all day long
While listening to the wild birds' song
Bye-bye pet it is time for me
To go and get some milk for tea

   God Bless
   Love Angie

A Pearson

HOMELESSNESS

He sits out there, so tired and drawn
Looks so sad, alone and forlorn
His grubby pet dog, by his side
Probably his only companion, in which to confide.

People walk past, they turn and stare
Laugh out loud at his untidy, matted grey hair
His boots are worn, his feet grow cold
Dreams of family, friends and laughter slowly unfold.

When it grows dark, he must sleep
Curl up in a ball, in an untidy heap
Toss and turn in his cardboard home
Feeling depressed, so extremely alone.

The winter closes in, and the nights are long
He has no-one, nowhere to belong
With only a thin rug to keep him warm
He must sit and wait patiently for the break of dawn.

Will anyone ever take pity on him
His clothes are ripped, he's dangerously thin
But still he sits and stares at you
Together, surely there is something we can do.

Lorraine Corden (15)

FEELINGS OF LOVE

You didn't see me, I saw you first
        across a room full of people
I couldn't take my eyes away from you
        you stood out from the crowd so slim and tall
A face with such a beautiful smile,
        that would make anyone's day
What could I do to make you notice me?
        if I went up to you, what would I say?
My heart was a-pounding I felt so weak
        just had to sit down before I fell
Yes I had fallen all right, fallen in love
        with *love*, I'm sure everyone could tell
All of a sudden you turned and looked over
        and gave me one of your beautiful smiles
Slowly you came across to me, the time you took
        and the distance seemed like miles
You said your name, but I barely heard, as
        I couldn't believe you were so near
What could I say now that you stood close by?
        I couldn't even see as I was blinded with
        every tear
You touched my chin and tilted my face
        and you saw what I couldn't hide
I knew you felt the same and would
        always be at my side.

Linda Roberts

ON LIFE'S FRAILTIES

Who is this tiny, frail person,
So fragile and delicate,
So easily moved to tears,
Sitting quietly beside her window,
In her own private world?

It seems such a little while
Since we climbed the heather-clad hills,
And swam in the icy waters
Of that lovely Scottish loch
All the long summer days,
And spent hours together
Beside the fire, reading,
Or talking, or playing Scrabble
When the nights drew in
And winter advanced.
It was a delightful companionship.
I thought nothing could touch it.

And now I wonder about you,
My other tiny, frail person,
Nestling so peacefully beside me.
Will you one day
Regret the passing of
Our delightful companionship,
As I slowly retreat
Into a world you cannot share?

Roslyn Lawrance

NO WAY BACK

This was their big day, the day they would visit the notary.
The Spanish sun rose like a ball of flame
And shafted across the bed ending their restless night,
They wondered, were they right? But hope chased doubt away.

It was nearly over, their furniture rested in a repository
Until it could be shipped out here to Spain.
Their little house had looked so neat and bright
Before the whirlwind sale took place last May.

That was the beginning of a short and hectic story.
Now, looking back, it seemed impossible to explain
How they could have loved the villa at first sight
And made a snap decision on that very day.

Living in Spain had not been considered seriously,
It was meant to be a holiday when they came
But they were quickly captivated by the light
And easy life in this environment of endless play.

The villa had a welcome touch of luxury,
The climate offered warmth instead of rain,
Good food and wine the palate to excite,
And sandy, sun-kissed beaches on which to lay.

The local Brits all viewed their lives complacently.
No worries, always summer, little pain,
But to their national customs they held tight
And occasionally let nostalgia hold full sway.

Just five short hours now before their legal foray,
After which the Escritura would be theirs to claim,
Then, no way back, whatever became their plight
Their future would lie in Spain where they must stay.

Hilda M Norden

SOUNDS

Some sounds are loud and crashing
Some are soft and sweet
Some set our feet a tapping
To the rhythm of a beat
Some set us on a journey
Through land or sea or sky
Or fill our hearts with wonder
As we hear a babe's first cry

Some sounds fill us with happiness
Others make us sad
Some we wish we'd never heard
They make us feel real bad
Some set our hearts a beating
Some take us by surprise
Some are soft and soothing
Or bring tears into our eyes

Some sounds bring warmth and comfort
Like the crackling of a fire
Or take our thoughts to heaven
As we listen to a choir
Some fill our hearts with love and joy
Give strength along the way
To most of us the sounds we hear
Affect us every day.

Dorothy Durrant

MOUNT CABURN

Blots of past
On crowded country
Wilderness Island
Semi-Rural Sea
Shaved grass and droppings
Small corner of a county
Promoted to forever
By me.

The Hill's a world
And the person on it
Self Sentinel unfurled

Who squats
And stares his hour upon its turf . . .

A cloud comes to rest.
Sitting in its belly
High up cloud
Low down fog.

Hiss of busy roundabout
Blade of grass shakes
Same thing.

Staring at the one
Reflecting on the truth
That is the Highway Code.

Staring at the other
Reflecting on the truth
That is the Air Code.

Staring at my watch
Reflecting on the truth
That is sunset.

Rising up
On the Downs.
Descending
On a high.

Newell Fisher

PAIN

Have you ever seen my pain,
a teenager just playing a stupid game.
Honestly he would never have knew,
what was going to pop up out of the blue.
His mates just pushed him go on go on,
Just steal the car you're doing no wrong.
And so he did he jumped into the car
He didn't drive it very far.
For a little girl got in his way
Just imagine the rest and remember he paid.
For the little girl slowly died
And her mum and dad cried and cried.
So remember when you're on the road
(Think safety that is the right code)

Ria Saunders (14)

ONE WOMAN MANY FACES

She sits by her mirror
Looking to see
What kind of person
She can be
A woman with pride
Is a woman with virtue
A woman who lied
Is a woman who's hurt you.

One woman many faces
One life so many places
She changes with time
Turns cruel when there's crime
Is giving with love
Makes peace like the dove.

This woman is not consistent
With the way her life must be
All it is, is metamorphosis
So why can't she see
That life itself is just a kiss
That cares for you and me
It's time to change her life to one
To face up to things and never run . . .

Helena Pavitt

HEART LIKE THUNDER

I can be as weak as you are strong
I can be as right as you are wrong
I can be foolish all along in love.

My heart is like the thunder
It will often make you wonder
How close it is before the rain.

I am sweet as I am sour
I can be barren or I may flower
I will never know my real ground.

All of my words and many of my doings
Are said and done because I like to play games
I'm not afraid to hurt anyone
But I wouldn't if I loved them
I can never take the pictures from their frames.

I am harmless or am I dangerous?
This world is far too strange for us
I'll never unite in its feel.

And my heart is like the thunder
It will always make you wonder
How far it is from the pain.

You may feast upon my hunger
As we're both not getting younger
I need all, I need nothing in love.

Stewart Lennox

OCEAN LIFE

East winds echo
  sounds of gulls above the beach
    Retreating waves carry
      sand and shingle beyond our reach,
        Morning mists hang
          cold and wet above the sea
            Tide beats against
              catching fish, - oh please, not me

Fishing vessels sail
  Above the watery world we know
    Nets close around
      seeking reward in the ocean below,
        Life swims away
          for a much greater need ashore
            Life exists again
              although man will still need more.

Stephen F Jeanes

INFORMATION

We hope you have enjoyed reading this book - and that you will continue to enjoy it in the coming years.

If you like reading and writing poetry drop us a line, or give us a call, and we'll send you a free information pack.

Write to

Anchor Books Information
1-2 Wainman Road
Woodston
Peterborough
PE2 7BU